THE LAST HERO

THE LAST HERO

The Gallant Story of
DONALD CAMPBELL
and the Land Speed Record—1964

by JOHN PEARSON

DAVID McKAY COMPANY, Inc.
New York

THE LAST HERO

Library of Congress Catalog Card Number: 66-10675

MANUFACTURED IN THE UNITED STATES OF AMERICA

VAN REES PRESS • NEW YORK

To

Tom Pearson

CHAPTER ONE

ADELAIDE in early May. The South Australian winter had almost begun. The big plane trees beside the parks were shedding their leaves, the beaches were emptying. After London it seemed a lonely, gentle, forgotten place. In the afternoons thick rain clouds would billow across the city as if a rubber factory had suddenly caught fire. It was impossible to find a taxi anywhere.

Reporters tell you May in South Australia is a bad time for news, but the papers seemed to have enough disaster and impending disaster to go around. There was to be a transport strike the following week unless someone did something about it. One of Sukarno's bombers had crashed in the Celebes with the loss of all six men aboard. Another vice probe was in full swing in Sydney. And there on the back page of the *Adelaide Advertiser* for Saturday, May 2nd, was all the latest about Campbell.

It was the sort of news appropriate for back pages of newspapers, with that big aerial photograph of that salt desert, Lake Eyre, under water and the car like the silhouette of some dismembered airplane fuselage, reflected forlornly in the middle of it.

It looked very dead.

"Bluebird of Unhappiness" was the headline in forty-eight-point type, for headline writers in Australia have as

1

much liberty to state the obvious as anywhere else in the free world. The reporter had done a neat burial job on poor Donald, too. There was an interview with him—very full, very fair, very sad.

"This is heartbreak, Donald Campbell said today as his trial runs were again postponed." Twenty-four points of water, over an inch, had fallen the night before the picture was taken, and he had already flown up and down the track inspecting the damage. In places there was still an inch of water. Once again his attempt on the record had ground to a halt.

I tried thinking of Campbell and his predicament up there, four hundred miles to the north, with his car and his camp of technicians and his flooded, solitary salt lake in the middle of the great Antipodean nowhere. Record-breaking is like revolution: success is its only excuse and failure diminishes everyone in contact with it.

I knew that Campbell had staked everything on this last throw of his, but back in London the idea of staking everything on something as essentially absurd as a racing record had seemed almost a joke. Even for him it had. I had heard him say it once or twice at parties when people asked him whether he was really going to do it this time.

"Well, I've put so much into it now, that it looks as if it will have to be my neck or the record." And he would wink at whoever had asked the question, and no one would know whether the wink was serious or not. Some people say he winks too much. He has very pale eyes, the lightest possible shade of blue. I could not imagine him winking at anyone up at Lake Eyre at the moment.

The only person I had met in Adelaide who knew him well was Florence. An old friend of the Campbells, she is tough, she is sentimental, and she runs the best nightclub in Adelaide. When she met me at the plane from Sydney she was suf-

2

fering from a mild attack of laryngitis, which gave all her news a curiously sepulchral quality. Only that morning she had got through by telephone to Campbell's wife, Tonia, up at the lake and learned that Campbell was planning to fly down to Adelaide on Sunday afternoon.

"Things sounded real rough," she croaked. "'*Real* rough. I just don't see how Donald can take another beating like this. They're all sitting around on the edge of that silly lake, and nobody knows whether the car can run or what they can do. Tonia says he's not sleeping well. It seems like the end of the road for him, though for God's sake, don't tell him I said so."

Florence looks like a cross between Judy Garland and a swimming instructress. She wore pink satin slacks and gold slippers to meet me, and the next day, although Adelaide is known as the city of churches, and although it was the Sabbath, she was wearing them again as she waited with me at the airport for Campbell's plane to arrive.

Adelaide has a clean, rather sleepy airport, and on Sunday afternoons it is particularly quiet, with large notices everywhere prohibiting the unauthorized transit of fruit from one state to another. Florence's laryngitis had improved, and while we waited I told her how Campbell had invited me to join his party and write the story of the record attempt.

We had met in the bar of the Dorchester Hotel in London and he had mentioned the idea quite suddenly.

"Why not come," he had said. "If you're interested in human nature in the raw you could do a lot worse than a record bid. No one's ever told the full story of one of these strange affairs. This might almost be one of the last of them, and I'd like it done while there's still a chance. Believe you me, it'll be something the like of which you'll never see again."

As I told Florence, she nodded as if she had heard all this

3

before. Instead of replying, she switched the subject and began telling me about her husband and how she was flying up to Surabaya in a few days for her divorce.

"He's a Norwegian sea captain. He's very good-looking and I'm fond of him. The only trouble is, we hardly ever seem to meet. I mean, when you even have to go to a place like Indonesia to get unhitched from your old man, there's not much future in the marriage, is there?"

Either the thought of her husband or the thought of leaving him seemed to cheer her up, and I asked her about Campbell.

"Attractive? Oh no, not attractive. Not Donald. Not in any *conventional* way." She shook her head. "Not to me anyhow, and perhaps that's just as well, since Tonia's a great friend of mine and I've booked her to sing at a gala night at the club when he's got the record. No, he's not sexy or anything like that, but he can be very exciting. Whenever I'm near him I get the feeling something's going to happen. Things always happen when Donald's around. That's for sure."

It was nearly 2:00 by then and there was no sign of a plane. I asked Florence whether she thought Campbell ever could get the record.

"He could. Mind you, he's an odd man and Lake Eyre's an odd place. Once you're in a place like that anything can happen. But I think the salt will dry out for him quicker than anyone thinks. Up where the track is, near the Simpson Desert, the sun's so hot it's been known to dehydrate the body of a man completely in a few hours. Every drop of moisture dried right out of him. Dry as a bone. That's how they find the body of anyone who gets lost up around Lake Eyre."

It was shortly after 2:00 that the afternoon Ansett plane roared down the silent runway with its load of vacationers returning from Kangaroo Island, and Florence spotted Campbell's plane circling in behind it. It was blue and white and looked very small. It had a high tail fin and seemed to hop down after the Ansett plane like some busy insect that had buzzed after it all the way from Kangaroo Island. The Ansett unloaded the weekenders with their suitcases and their sunburn and their large healthy children, and then I saw Campbell.

He was walking across the tarmac with a blue leather overnight case, the same small, rather jaunty man I remembered from London. He had the same raffish air, the same navy blue blazer with the Bluebird buttons. He was wearing one of the shirts he has specially made for him, a particular shade of Bluebird blue, by a firm in Jermyn Street. Tonia walked quietly by his side.

"Well, he *looks* all right," said Florence.

But when I went out to meet him, I saw that he had changed. His face was thinner and grayer than when I saw him last. The tendons of his neck were showing. He had had a terrible haircut.

"How are you feeling?" I asked.

"Not much use for anything really, old sport. Not much use." He had a faint stammer I had never noticed before, and his defeat seemed total and inescapable. He had a particular look I remembered from the wartime newsreels of pilots who had been shot down and escaped with nothing but their lives.

But this was only the start. For on May 3rd, in the second week of his attempt on the land speed record of the world, Donald Campbell still had not driven his car.

Campbell's haggard appearance was not caused only by the hammering he had had up at the lake. On the face of it he should have been able to take a setback like this in his

5

stride. Already he held more world speed records than any man alive, and he had not won them easily.

In one of his earliest attempts on the water speed record in 1951 on Lake Coniston, his propeller-driven Bluebird boat hit a submerged log at speed and had to be completely scrapped. Soon after this, John Cobb had been killed on Loch Ness when his boat Crusader was shaken to pieces by high-frequency vibrations at a speed of around 200 miles an hour. The death of the imperturbable Cobb, who already held the world land speed record of 394.4 miles an hour, seemed to show the folly of everything Campbell was attempting. People began to speak of a mysterious water barrier that would destroy any boat at these unexplored speeds.

But Campbell had gone on. With two young designers, Lewis and Ken Norris, who had just formed their own small firm of consulting engineers near Brighton, he had built a revolutionary jet-propelled hydroplane, and on July 23, 1955, at Ulswater, this new Bluebird broke through the water barrier that had killed Cobb and set up a new water speed record of 202 miles an hour.

Nevertheless, Campbell's reputation for bad luck continued. Two months later he went to Lake Mead in Nevada to establish a new water speed record in America, and Bluebird sank on the first attempt. He and his team had to raise it and completely overhaul it before he could push the record up to 216 miles an hour.

This second record of his was the high spot of his career. The Foreign Office congratulated him. The Queen decorated him. The Las Vegas Chamber of Commerce presented him with a vast and untarnishable gold pot, which stands today in the hall of his Surrey mansion recording "the courage and scientific achievement of Donald Campbell in raising the world speed record to 216 miles an hour on the waters of

6

.Lake Mead and so showing the possibilities of the lake as an area of aquatic recreation."

But success at Lake Mead was also the start of the trouble that was to culminate at Lake Eyre. It was the beginning of his dream of becoming the fastest man on land as well as on water.

Possibly it was all an enormous mistake. All his experience as a record-breaker had been on water, and he had never driven so much as an ordinary racing car at speed. Also it was arguable that by then the days of the big record-breaking car were already over, that the conventional car had been driven nearly as fast as it ever would, and that in the age of space exploration few people cared whether Cobb's record stood or fell.

But if Donald Campbell's decision in 1955 to build a record-breaking car was a mistake, it was a mistake in the grandest possible manner. The car he planned was to be even more revolutionary than his boat. It would be driven through its fifty-two-inch tires by a specially adapted airplane gas turbine developing over five thousand brake horsepower. It would be constructed like the body of a plane and have mechanical brakes designed to operate at 400 miles an hour plus. The car was stressed to withstand a total load of thirty tons on the suspension. Campbell has a touch of extravagance to his nature, which reflected in his plans for the car. Typically, it was going to be the fastest, the most sophisticated, the most finely calculated car in the world.

From this moment on, Bluebird became the center of Campbell's life. Four more times he raised the water speed record on Lake Coniston, but building his car had become his real career and his obsession. His reputation depended on it. All his money was involved in it. And the way Campbell inspired and cajoled more than seventy leading British firms to contribute to it must rank as one of the most remarkable off-beat selling jobs in postwar Britain.

Campbell is rarely punctual. He lacks tact. He hates writing letters. He gets bored easily with people and has an inexplicable, almost animal capacity for arousing violent antipathy at sight in quite unlikely individuals. Yet this was the man who inspired the giant British Petroleum oil company to back him to the tune of "something in the vicinity of a quarter of a million pounds," until the break came at the end of 1963. The Dunlop Rubber Company, oldest and best-known of the British tire manufacturers, built a special two-hundred-thousand-pound test plant primarily so that Bluebird could have the tires it needed. (The plant, of course, has since been used to test other high-speed tires.) The big Girling Brake Company developed a special form of brake for Bluebird. The Lucas Electrical Company, Britain's largest electrical automobile equipment manufacturer, backed Campbell for Bluebird's complex circuits. And still another industrial giant, the Smith's Industrial Instruments Company, developed Bluebird's instrumentation.

The actual car, excluding its components, cost around thirty-five thousand pounds to build, but it is difficult to make a realistic guess at how much the Bluebird project as a whole has consumed. Record bids by their very nature are expensive things to mount, especially when they take place around the other side of the world, and there was nothing small about the scale of Campbell's operations.

Five British companies supported the record attempt with cash. Many additional companies supplied components for Bluebird free of cost. Some of these components were intricate and expensive, others comparatively minor, involving costs on the order of fifteen to twenty pounds.

And that afternoon in Adelaide, when Campbell had flown down from Lake Eyre with disaster written all over his face,

8

every penny invested in Bluebird had still to pay off. His reputation, which he had staked personally to the head of each of the seventy companies, was still in the balance. Some said it was bad luck. Others were less polite. But the fact was that Bluebird was still untried and Campbell had yet to prove himself and the car.

In 1960 Bluebird should have won the record at Utah. Instead it crashed at 360 miles an hour. Campbell suffered a broken right eardrum, a ruptured middle ear, a basal skull fracture, and a contusion of the brain. But he held a press conference at his hospital in Salt Lake City three weeks after the crash to announce that he would try again when he was better. Sir Alfred Owen, the Bible-loving Birmingham millionaire industrialist, was impressed. "If Campbell has the guts to have another go," he said, "I'll build him another car." Campbell cabled his acceptance and the idea of a second Bluebird was born.

This was the car lapping the water of Lake Eyre now. A large tail fin had been added to cut down the risk of a repetition of the Utah crash, but basically it was built to the same design as the original Bluebird.

For Campbell the 1963 record bid in Australia had been the disaster to end all disasters. He and the Bluebird project were already on trial and everything imaginable had gone wrong. The Australian press had crucified him. The rains had come and flooded the lake. He was still suffering from the aftereffects of his injuries, and when the attempt was finally called off in the middle of May, all Campbell's hopes, all those brave intentions from the days of Lake Mead had collapsed in a welter of lawsuits and recriminations. Stirling Moss held a special press conference to announce that in his opinion Campbell was not up to driving the car. "He lacks," said Moss, "the necessary split-second reactions of a Grand Prix racing driver."

9

There had been disagreements in the camp over an employee from the Owen organization, which ended with public accusations from Sir Alfred that the failure to get the record was due to mismanagement by Campbell. Campbell sued. Sir Alfred withdrew. The two men were seen shaking hands on television. "When two gentlemen shake hands after a quarrel," Campbell told an interviewer, "that's the end of the matter."

But the sour mood that the whole incident left behind settled like a damp fog over the entire Bluebird project. By 1964 no further British backers were forthcoming, and Campbell's beneficial relationship with British industry seemed almost over. British Petroleum had made any further association conditional on Campbell's accepting a company nominee as manager of the Bluebird project, and for him this was unthinkable.

So this final trip to Australia had been almost entirely at his own expense. Some of his previous supporters like Bristol Siddeley, Girling, Smith's Instruments, and the Owen organization had sent specialist engineers to help maintain the car when it was running. But there was no cash. The only big financial support Campbell had this time was from Ampol, an all-Australian oil company that was paying him an undisclosed sum for the right to allow Bluebird to run on their fuel (and, more important, the right to say so in the advertisements). Once the record was won, this sum would be doubled, and three of the English companies with components in Bluebird had promised substantial bonuses for their advertising rights. Without a record this time, Campbell knew he could never hope to cover his expenses.

But there was more than mere money at stake. There was the myth he was trying to live up to and the sort of man he was trying to be.

In some ways he was the last person in the world to be expected to undertake anything as complex and cold-blooded as modern record-breaking. He had a bad medical history. As a child he had rheumatic fever, which had caused him to be invalided out of the R.A.F. during the war after he had been accepted for pilot training. The head injuries at Utah had added to his troubles. He is not an easy man to deal with. He is prickly. He is emotional. He is unpredictable. He is superstitious. Above all, he is the son of his father, Sir Malcolm Campbell, and throughout his life he has had to live in the shadow of the most successful record-breaker of all time.

When he died in his bed in 1948 at the age of sixty-four, Sir Malcolm Campbell had held the land speed record nine times and the water speed record three times. He had been knighted by George V after recovering the world land speed record for Britain at Daytona Beach in 1931, and he had died rich. Apart from the money made from record-breaking, he had been a successful insurance broker at Lloyds, and his will revealed that he had left more than a quarter of a million pounds.

But as well as a financial success, Sir Malcolm Campbell had been a character. Tough, lean, sharp-eyed, he was part of the fabric of the Thirties. He was an amateur and a gentleman. All his success had come at a time when the world still wanted heroes like him. He had started racing at Brooklands as a sport and had managed to keep it a sport until the end. This was a great achievement, for in those early days, before speed became a branch of science fiction, he was living proof that the machinery had not yet got out of hand. The human element still counted for something. The man was superior to the machine and he was the man.

He had first called one of his cars Bluebird after Maeterlinck's play, and long after the play was forgotten Campbell and Bluebird were still there. Already mathematicians were taking speed to a point where it was meaningless to the lay-drove their cars as in earlier days they drove their coaches.

Sir Malcolm was lucky in the way the Thirties treated its heroes. Today fame is like one of those selective weed killers that destroys a plant by making it grow too fast and exhausting it. Not so when he was alive. He tended his fame with careful sense and was a celebrity all his days.

But Sir Malcolm had died at the end of an era. Now at Lake Eyre Donald Campbell was still trying to continue where his father had left off.

Campbell spent only one night in Adelaide. He stayed with friends on the outskirts of the city and said he slept well. Monday morning he spent shopping, buying stores needed up at the lake—a dozen extra flashlights, several pairs of desert boots, a parka, blankets, a couple of bottles of liniment—but he was anxious to get back to the lake, and we left Adelaide airport on Monday afternoon at 2:36 P.M. South Australia time in a twin-engined Aero Commander that Campbell had chartered specially for the attempt.

There was an eight-mile-an-hour wind from the southwest, but the weather forecast was good all the way through to Alice Springs, and once we had watched the afternoon DC-3 sail off behind us to Melbourne we had the sky to ourselves.

Campbell is a good pilot. He looks right in a cockpit just as he looks wrong behind a desk, and he is a surprisingly meticulous flier.

"The one place you'll never catch me fooling around is in the air," he said as he repeated his speed and height back to the flight controller at Adelaide.

Adelaide is at the bottom of a long wedge of sea driven up toward the middle of Australia. At some time in the past the tip of the wedge connected with a chain of lakes still farther north, and Lake Eyre and Lake Torrens had both emptied in-man. Already what counted was not the man in the cockpit but the scientists in the laboratories and the skill with which their missiles were launched.

But while Sir Malcolm had been inching his speeds up in battles with men like Segrave and Parry Thomas, none of this seemed to matter, and he had still been part of an older, more comprehensible tradition where sporting aristocrats to the sea. There had been forests then and heavy rainfall. Twenty thousand years ago Lake Eyre was still part of a much larger fresh-water lake called Lake Dieri. There were crocodiles at that time and large fish, and giant marsupials roamed the forests.

All this was matter now for the geologists. Slowly the river connecting the lakes with the sea had silted up and died, and with it died the whole of the flat, rich forest land around. As the lakes lost their outlet and the waters went on evaporating, their salinity increased. The fish and the crocodiles vanished. The forests fell. The great marsupials died. And as the rainfall diminished, the whole area withered into the hot, dry desert that was our destination.

Although it continued to drain the water from a quarter of Australia, Lake Eyre died, too. With each century that passed, the evaporation of the rivers flowing into it built up the layers of its salt, the salt on which Campbell was hoping to win his record.

It was a long flight, taking nearly the entire afternoon, and from six thousand feet the whole prehistory of this strange country lay stretched below. We passed Port Pirie where the railhead touches the coast, where freshly mined iron ore is brought and shipped down to Adelaide. The long purple scar of the Flinders range was on the right, and ahead lay the mauve and brown emptiness of Australia's dead heart.

It was at 4:20 that we saw the first pale glint on the horizon like the sun striking a thin strip of steel, and Campbell pointed and shouted, "There! There she is. There's the lake. We'll fly over. We've just time before dusk."

The sun was almost down before we were there and the lake looked as flat and dead as a sheet of asbestos.

"We'll go down," Campbell shouted above the racket of the motors. "See how the surface is since we left." And as the engines whined and the vertigo caught us and we spiraled our way down to within a few hundred feet of the surface, layer upon layer of color began to appear, greens and yellows, silvers and pinks and browns, until it was like descending into the heart of a freshly opened oyster.

Campbell was enjoying himself. He was grinning now and shouting with excitement as he pulled the plane out of its turn and pointed down to where a narrow black speck lay like a matchstick on the strange surface of the lake.

"That's the car. That's Bluebird. She's still there." And we came in lower still until we could see the outline of the steel ribs under the green canvas of the hangar where the car was housed and the guy ropes of the tents where the mechanics kept the spares.

There were a couple of trucks and a pile of oil drums and a thin, silver-latticed radio mast. But there was no sign of life. The camp looked derelict. It could have been there for years like the headquarters of an expedition that lost its way.

Due north ran a narrow line, as straight and precise as if ruled in pink crayon across the salt, and twice we flew over it.

"That's the track," said Campbell. "Fifteen miles of it. Six months to prepare. Five hundred pounds a mile in preparation costs. That's where we run—when we run."

His wife asked him what he thought of the surface of the salt.

"Not bad, not bad at all. It's certainly dried out a lot in a couple of days. The wind shifts it, you know. Actually blows

14

the water from one side of the lake to the other, and it looks as though we might have been lucky."

He pointed far over to the eastern shore where there was a dark blotch along the whole edge of the salt, like the mark hot milk leaves behind when it spills on a carpet.

"That's last Friday's rain. Let's just hope it evaporates before the wind changes its mind and blows it back into the center of the track."

The flight across the lake had put us behind schedule, and Campbell began to worry about the dark, for the runway had no flare path. Muloorina, the sheep station where Campbell and all the main party were living, was thirty-five miles away, and he seemed to think we would be only just in time.

Nightfall in the outback is swift and spectacular, and the first stars were already out. The land was blurred with shadows as the wheels rasped down on the landing strip and the propellers reversed with a whirring of air and the motor surged for the last time and was still.

"Muloorina," said Campbell. "We've arrived."

I had no idea what I was stepping into as I left the plane. After the roar of the motors, the sudden silence was intense. There was gravel underfoot and a great cloud of dust from the landing was beginning to settle. Two boys were there to watch us as we pulled our bags from the luggage compartment. They rode off on old bicycles without a word. A wind pump was slowly turning at the end of the runway, and beyond was a long corrugated iron roof, silhouetted against the glow of sunset.

We walked toward it. The silence was complete, and in the dusk the smell of the outback was on the wind, an old smell—dry, dusty, faintly aromatic. Then people came out to meet us, but they were indistinct in that half light.

"Hi, Don." "Welcome back, Skipper." "What're the girls like now in civilization?"

The voices sounded strange in the darkness and emptiness.

"Not a bad trip, Unc," I heard Campbell say. "I got you a few cans of that Dunhill mixture. How's the lake?"

"So-so, Skipper. So-so."

Even this close it was too dark to distinguish faces clearly, and all I could see of the man Campbell was talking to was a short stocky figure and an old trilby hat with the brim turned down. Campbell put his arm round the man's shoulder as they walked toward one of the bungalows beyond. There was a big yard with a row of sheds on the other side. The lights were on and someone was slaughtering a sheep. The hind legs were tied to a beam, and there was no noise as it had its throat cut.

CHAPTER TWO

"HELLO, Elliot. Elliot, you old devil. Where are you? We've a new arrival. Is there a bed for him on the verandah or does he have to sleep with the girls?" Campbell let the screen door of the bungalow slam behind him, and the yellow moths that clung to it fluttered up against the light. An old dog with a ginger tail woke to see what all the fuss was about.

"Steady now, Donald. Steady," said a voice from a door on the other side of the verandah. "I'm not so young as I used to be, and with all your men here I've had a busy day of it."

"So that's where you're hiding," said Campbell, and still laden with his knapsack and his liniment and his cans of Dunhill tobacco, he led the way into a long, brightly lit sitting room with a blue-and-pink-flowered carpet on the floor, a player piano against the far wall, and vases of plastic lilacs on the mantelpiece. Resplendent in a big green armchair was the man Campbell was looking for.

He was short and very solid with thick gray hair and mahogany-colored arms. He wore wide, red-striped suspenders and a precise mustache that gave his weather-beaten face a touch of quite extraordinary wickedness.

"This," said Campbell, "is the king. Elliot Price, King of Muloorina."

"That's right," he said. "Except for the lake. That's not in

17

my territory. In the state it's in now, I'll let you be King of Lake Eyre, Donald."

"How is the course?" asked Campbell quickly. "When we flew over it just now it didn't look too bad."

"Well, Donald, I've been here twenty-one years and I still don't understand that bloody lake. Last year before you came it had a surface like concrete. Then you had your rain. Soon as you arrived, if you remember."

"Yes," said Campbell grimly, "I remember."

"First rain it had had for eight years. Now it starts again, soon as you turn up, for the second year running. I don't understand these things, Donald, and I can't say I want to. All I do know is that when I first came here the natives would never have anything to do with the lake. Wouldn't go near the place. And the black fellows have their reasons for these things. So you can have it, Donald. I'll stick to my sheep. Sheep's chancey things, but I still prefer them."

"Well, if I do as well out of the lake as you've done out of your sheep, Elliot, I shan't do too badly."

"P'raps, Donald," said the old man, smiling to himself and shaking his head. "We'll see."

"What d'you mean, we'll see?" said Campbell, suddenly anxious to change the subject. "How much are you worth, Elliot? Let's have the truth. Have you made your million yet?"

"Now, Donald," said the old man, yawning and scratching his chest, "that'd be telling, and to be truthful I'm not sure of the answer myself. We've enough to be comfortable. I've got the plane and the new Buick for myself. I run twelve thousand sheep, and all the money I get goes back into the business. There's fourteen miles of inch-and-a-quarter plastic piping for me waiting to be collected in the goods yard at Marree at the moment. Fourteen miles at two shillings a foot, work it out for yourself. That's where the money goes."

18

And this was where much of Elliot Price's money had been going from the day toward the end of 1942 when he arrived at Muloorina with a thousand pounds and an old Dennis truck. He was forty-one and had made his living until then as a traveling well-driller. It was because he reckoned he could find water near Muloorina that he had gambled all his savings and settled his family on this forgotten strip of desert bordering on the southern shores of Lake Eyre.

When he came he had found a deserted homestead dating back to the days when this part of Australia had been used to breed the camels whose ancestors had been imported from Afghanistan for the great journeys of exploration across Australia in the eighteen-seventies. For years the camel trails had passed this way, northeast along the Birdsville track, skirting the parched desert lands toward Alice Springs and beyond.

Then the trucks had taken over, and in batches of forty and fifty at a time the camels, like obsolescent machines, had been brought to Muloorina to be destroyed. When Elliot Price arrived at Muloorina he found great piles of camel bones around the homestead. Being an economical man, he had used them to mark out his airstrip.

This common sense was typical of him and the way he took this dead land and put it to his own uses. He drilled for water, and with the thirteenth shaft he found it as he said he would. He also discovered the tough, water-bearing roots and the lichens and succulents that could keep a sheep alive on land that might go without rain for five years in succession. And he and his children and their children in their turn had built Muloorina into a family kingdom over which Elliot Price ruled like the head of some feudal dynasty.

It was a kingdom he had kept jealously within his family. Each of his married children had a bungalow within walking distance of the main homestead building, and in his cellars Price kept sufficient stores to last the whole community six months. The South Australian government supplied a teacher who ran a school in which every pupil was a Price grandchild.

"You know what I've been doing today, Donald?" said the old man later as he got up to go in to supper. "Been choosing a spot for my grave. Finally settled on that bit of rising ground beside the track from Marree where you first catch sight of the homestead. When you get to my age you worry about these things. I want a big stone there, so in years to come, when they've built a proper road out here, people will stop and ask what the bloody great stone's for, and someone'll say, 'that's where they buried the old bastard who started it all!' "

He buttoned the neck of his shirt and began pulling an ancient gray jacket over his bull-like shoulders.

"I know it's silly, but these things come to matter, Donald. They matter a lot."

"I know they do, Elliot," Campbell replied softly. "I know."

Perhaps it was the influence of Elliot Price that produced the distinctly feudal air all the meals at Muloorina seemed to share. The men sat together at a long table, with Price enthroned at one end in a large wooden armchair. Campbell, in a slightly smaller one, sat at the other.

This male, tribal world suited Campbell. His face lost the lines, the grayness of Adelaide. Now that he was back among people he knew and trusted, the record bid was no longer the ordeal of a lonely man. It was what it always should have been—an adventure to be shared, and the more people who joined in the better.

It was interesting to watch him at dinner that first evening. Leo Villa, Campbell's chief engineer, was on his left, a solid, avuncular presence in a khaki shirt. He was the man wearing

20

the trilby hat who had been waiting for us that night on the runway, and he was an important part of the whole Campbell legend. For Leo Villa was not merely Campbell's engineer; he was his friend, his conscience, and his most important link with the past. If Campbell was Quixote, Villa was Sancho Panza. He had joined Sir Malcolm Campbell as mechanic when he was twenty-three, and had been with the family ever since. Campbell still called him "Unc." He had built the Bluebird car of 1935—the first car to reach 300 miles an hour—with his own hands, and he had more first-hand experience of record-breaking than any man alive. He is the sort of man who never changes, and it was inevitable that when Sir Malcolm died he should have carried on his life's work with the son.

Opposite Villa sat Ken Norris, the third key man in the Bluebird team. He held a degree in aeronautical engineering from Imperial College, London, and with his brother Lewis had designed both the car and the record-breaking Bluebird jet boat. At one time his company had twenty people working on the designs for the car, and put in a total of thirty-six thousand design hours. A slim, determined man, whose nose was already peeling from the harsh sun of the outback, he ate less than either Campbell or Villa. Norris has a habit of answering direct technical questions by working out impromptu sums on stamp-sized pieces of paper. But he needed no calculations to answer the one question Campbell slipped in quite casually while the soup was still on the table.

"Is the car ready?"

"Had a look at her this morning. As far as we could see she was fine."

"And how was the salt?"

"Well, that's more difficult to be precise about." He pushed his hair back across his forehead and looked at Campbell, smiling a faint noncommittal smile that could have meant anything. "Ask Leo. He's the salt expert."

"Always hard to say on this lake," said Villa. The soup was very good and he was halfway through his second plateful. He enjoys his food, and the sunburned dome of his head gleamed benevolently above his spectacles. "The water's gone from the surface for the first few miles of the track, but I wouldn't like to say how hard the salt is, Skipper. And I wouldn't like to give my guarantee for the middle of that track of yours. I know Andrew Mustard has put a hell of a lot of work into it, but I've always had my doubts."

"You have, have you, Unc?" said Campbell. "Where is Andrew, incidentally?"

"Still down in Adelaide. He should be back tomorrow or the day after."

"Ah," said Campbell.

Now that he was here everyone seemed to have come alive, for he has an undeniable way with him, the same quality his father is said to have had, of entering a room and making himself the focus of everyone's attention.

"I don't know what you and your boys are thinking of doing with yourselves while the lake dries out," said Price suddenly. "But I'm planning to go up towards Cooper's Creek, baiting for dingoes. If you and any of the boys'd like to come along for the ride, Donald, you'd all be more'n welcome."

"Dingo baiting?" said someone. "How d'you do that, Elliot?"

"You poisons the bastards. Strychnine in kangaroo meat. You puts it down the burrows."

"But why poison them? Why not shoot them?" said Campbell.

"Takes too long and they're too hard to hit. You ever tried hitting a dingo, Don? Christ, they're smart, are dingoes. And beautiful. The most beautiful bastard creature you could hope to see, a well-fed dingo. And intelligent. The stories I could tell you about dingoes. But them's the biggest foul killers in the country. They'll tear the guts out of a couple of dozen sheep, one after the other, just for the fun of it."

The old man paused, elbows on table, to take a good mouthful of his own mutton.

"That's why you poisons 'em. So's I say, Donald, if you or your boys feels like a day or two up by Cooper's, you're more'n welcome. It's interesting country up there. You heard of Burke an' Wills, the explorers—it's right near where they died."

"Well, it's kind of you, Elliot, but I think we'll all be having work to do tomorrow."

As Campbell said this, I saw Leo Villa look up sharply, and for a moment it seemed as if he would speak. But he kept quiet and Campbell went on.

"One thing I wanted to ask you, Elliot. Earlier this evening you were talking about the lake and the way the aborigines would never go near it. What did you mean?"

"Oh, nothing, Don. They have these funny ideas of theirs. Forget it."

"But damn it, Elliot, this is your country. Just tell me about this lake. You know what happened last year as well as I do. It hadn't rained there for eight years. Then the night the army finished building the causeway for us, what happened? The heavens opened. Fine, we said, it's an exception, a freak. The lake dried out and we got ready to run on May 8th. And on the night of May 7th what happened again? Once more the heavens opened, and we were washed out. Now this year, Elliot, everyone told us there couldn't possibly be rain two years running. The chances of it happening were God knows how many hundred to one. And yet we come, we get ready to run, and then last Friday night the same thing happens. So what about that?"

23

Price seemed in two minds over what to reply.

"Well, you know how it is, Don. The aborigine can understand things we can't. They say their witch doctor can make rain or cause drought. He can put the finger on someone and two days later he's dead. No one knows how. There's no mark on the body. He's just dead. Well," and he paused to belch before continuing, "the lake has always been considered a place of death by the aborigines. They won't go on it and have always warned the white man not to. It's a sort of legend here. But you don't want to take any notice of that sort of nonsense. Superstition's all right for these ignorant simple bastards, but of course there's nothing in it. We've all been on the lake, haven't we? Yet we're still here."

Leo Villa had a box of fifty small Manila cheroots, and there was silence as he passed them round the table. All Campbell's attention seemed to be concentrated on his cigar. He moistened the end, snipped it deftly with a small steel cutter, and waited until the match he was lighting it with had nearly burned to his fingers before drawing his first puff.

"Unc, how long did Andrew Mustard say he would be staying down in Adelaide?"

"Till Wednesday, Skipper. He said in the state the lake's in at the moment it would be impossible to have a run before then."

"He did, did he? Well, that's a pity, because I think we're going to have a go tomorrow morning."

The promise of action was the most precious gift Campbell had to offer, and that evening I had the first taste of the weird excitement that was to build up and then vanish so many times in the weeks ahead.

Remember the isolation of the place, the silence of the nights, and the slowness with which day was to succeed day.

24

Remember the loneliness and the feeling the outback can give that you are becalmed, helpless in an ocean of desert. With all this, the promise of each new run with the car was the one drug that could make this place tolerable.

But that first night the excitement was highest, and incidents stick in the memory in a way they never did afterward. There was Leo Villa taking Campbell into the kitchen and sitting him down with a cup of tea at the long table covered with green and white checked oilcloth, and telling him how dangerous the rain-softened salt was still likely to be.

When Villa gets excited his spectacles mist up, and he talks very fast as if he were back in the pits at Brooklands snatching a few seconds before his driver slams in the clutch and roars off again around the track.

"But Don, listen. It's crazy trying anything on that track tomorrow. We don't know what it's like. Anything could happen on it. We just don't know."

The situation was clearly one Campbell had been facing with Villa on and off through most of his life, and he was very calm, very reasonable with him. He put a lot of sugar in his tea and waited for the old man to finish.

"Well, Unc," he said, "if we don't know we've just got to find out, haven't we?" And he smiled his most reassuring smile and put his hand on his friend's shoulder and winked, and Leo knew, from long experience, that there was nothing else to be said.

Later there was a briefing in one of the corrugated iron sheds used by the sheep shearers. Everyone remotely connected with the record bid was there, crammed into that bare, uncomfortable room with its scuffed concrete floor, its pile of mattresses in the corner, and its single light bulb shaded with the cover of a five-year-old copy of *Time* magazine.

There was Cliff Brebner, the gaunt amiable superintendent

from the South Australian police, who was responsible for security and communications with the lake. There was Tom Scrimshire, a large florid man, son of a butcher, who had been foreman in charge of building the car at Motor Panels. There were the technical experts—Carl Noble from Electro-Hydraulics, a former Navy pilot; Ken Reaks from Smith's Industrial Instruments, another former pilot; George Hammond from Bristol Siddeley, the big aircraft engine combine, who was responsible for Bluebird's Proteus turbine, and Tom Lawson and Ron Willies of Girling, who had helped develop the car's brakes.

All of them were personally involved in the car's failure or success. Each of them knew that his reputation and the reputation of his firm could suffer badly if anything went wrong at speed that could later be traced to his particular components.

And as well as the technical experts, there were the drivers and men who had been working on the track. Their faces, tanned and roughened by nearly a whole summer laboring up on the lake, made the white faces of the engineers appear delicate, almost feminine, by contrast. Even then, that first night, there seemed something skeptical, unimpressed about the way they listened as Campbell, another of Leo Villa's cigars between his lips, outlined the plans for the next morning's run.

"It will be in the nature of a test, gentlemen. A test for the car and a test for me. But primarily a test for the track. Frankly, no one knows how much damage last Friday night's rain has done, and the only way to find out is to do what I intend to do tomorrow morning."

On occasions such as these Campbell is at his best—crisply articulate, very sure of himself, like an actor who has really learned his lines and is beginning to enjoy his part. He was wearing a blue Eisenhower jacket with the red, white, and blue badge of the Ampol oil company on his left breast pocket.

The only questions that evening came from the one member of the Australian press to arrive so far. His name was Parr, Wally Parr, of the Australian Associated Press. He had a large brown notebook and was wearing denim overalls. He had the air of a man who was expecting trouble of one sort or another. He asked serious, factual questions, and had clearly been through the cuttings before he arrived.

"How much power will you be using, Donald?"

"That depends on what Ken Norris advises once he has seen the conditions. Probably thirty percent of maximum."

"That could take you up to what speed?"

"Around 280 to 300."

"And there is no significance in the absence of Andrew Mustard?"

"No, Wally. Andrew decided to have a day or two with his family down in Adelaide and will be back tomorrow or the day after."

But the most memorable face of all that night before the first run was not at the meeting in the shearers' quarters. It belonged to Campbell's wife, Tonia, and when we returned from the meeting, she was alone in the sitting room at the homestead.

It was just after 11:00, and the Prices and the rest of the family were asleep already. In the dining room beyond the swing doors with the frosted glass, her husband was now discussing the car's probable performance with its chief designer. Sheets of graph paper were scattered across the brown felt table cover. Norris had his slide rule, Campbell his pipe, and although the doors were closed the low buzz of their voices could be heard from where she was sitting.

But she took no notice. All her attention was on her embroidery, a small needlework picture of a South Sea island, and she worked deftly, methodically, a determined woman, used to taking trouble to get what she wanted.

She is Flemish. Her father owns a large hotel near Ostend. She is tall and has the sort of good looks that make mere prettiness somehow irrelevant. That evening she had taken charge of the kitchen and done most of the cooking. Soup was her specialty. Slowly the leaves of a small palm tree were taking shape from her needle.

"You're not seeing the real man here at all, you know," she said, nodding in the direction of the dining room. "These last few months have been hell for all of us, him particularly."

She went on sewing, and the buzz of conversation from the dining room continued.

"I wish to God he wouldn't do it. I admire him for it. Tremendously. I admire people who won't give in. But I wish it was all happening to somebody else's husband. You see, this is his life. Everything he stands for and believes in is at stake in this thing.

"He's a strange man, you know," she went on. "He's very brave and very superstitious and very tender. And if you want to understand him you really have to begin with his father."

She stopped sewing, and pulled her thick pink angora sweater around her, for the room was suddenly cold. The gold slippers she wore made a discreet protest against the overstuffed green armchairs and brown bulk of the piano.

"Was the soup all right tonight?" she asked. "The trouble with this place is the onions. Have you seen a good onion since you've been in Australia?"

CHAPTER THREE

THERE is a small, extremely rare albino lizard, about four inches long with pink eyes and a furtive manner. It is not an attractive animal. Until it moves it looks as if it has been pressed from white plastic. When it is startled its tail drops off.

But this lizard is unique. It has succeeded where men and all other animals have failed. It has learned to live on the surface of Lake Eyre, feeding, as far as one can discover, on flies and small insects that get blown onto the salt.

Normally you never see it, even after months on the lake, for its grubby white skin blends in perfectly with the grubby white surface of the salt. Why, during the course of its evolution it should have bothered to camouflage itself in this way, must remain one of the minor puzzles of zoology. For this lizard has no known competitors in its battle for existence. Until Campbell arrived it was the only thing to have found a use for this four thousand miles of salty nothingness.

At various times, it is true, the lizards are challenged in their possession of the lake, but not for long. Occasionally rabbits appear from nowhere and flock onto it, struggling over the soft mud that lines the shores like a treacherous brown moat. Ducks and parrots have been found there. Fat brown grasshoppers are sometimes blown onto it in the thousands by the great, dust-bearing winds that come sweeping across from the desert.

Men have tried to challenge the lizards, too. In the eighteen-forties and -fifties, after Edward John Eyre first viewed the lake and gave it his name, Lake Eyre became one of the great Australian mysteries, which later explorers set themselves to solve. One of them reported cliffs and fresh water there. Another insisted these were merely mirages. Another said it was surrounded by meadows of rich grass.

It was not until the end of the century that the truth about Lake Eyre was known and the geologists began to discover that this immense salt bed was the focus of a great internal drainage system for half a million square miles of central Australia.

But even then there was no certainty about the place. Were there minerals to be mined? Was there oil? No one knew. The explorers were succeeded by aerial surveys, and the aerial surveys by drilling rigs from the Department of Mines. It was estimated that the lake contained four hundred million tons of salt and that its surface varied between 39 and 29.2 feet below sea level. Investigation showed that in places the salt crust was up to fifteen inches thick. Beneath that was mud, thick, black, primeval mud, and as the trial drills of the geologists probed downward through it they brought up mineral specimens of considerable variety. There was gypsum and mica, palygorskite and montmorillonite. Kaolin and goethite appeared at a depth of 145 feet and alunite between 153 and 156 feet.

It was all very interesting, but it was not what the Department of Mines was looking for. The drilling rigs departed and the lizards once again were left in peace.

It was in 1961 that Campbell came for the first time. After his car had crashed on the salt flats at Utah, he had decided that for his next record bid he would have to find somewhere else, somewhere longer, smoother, flatter and less crowded. At Utah in 1960 the track had been a mere ten and a half miles; the surface had been made treacherous by the oil from other cars, and he had been under the constant pressure of having other speed trials going on throughout the time he was there. Any of these factors could have contributed to the crash. And none of them was likely to worry him on Lake Eyre.

He had heard about Lake Eyre through British Petroleum, which was still retaining him in those days, and in the spring he had flown out from Britain specially to see this mysterious lake, which only the largest atlases bothered to record. It had been a nightmare journey for him. He was still suffering the aftereffects of the crash, and in San Francisco he had had a nervous attack so severe that he nearly called off the entire visit. Instead he took two sleeping pills, and the Qantas manager at the airport arranged for him to travel the rest of the way in the crew bunk.

A representative of British Petroleum met him at the airport at Adelaide. By then the attack was over. Campbell borrowed a hat with a wide brim and flew to Muloorina the following day. As soon as he saw the lake he knew he had found what he wanted. "I could hardly believe it," he says. "The surface was like concrete. It was flat, it was smooth, and it seemed to go on forever."

He had flown up with several companions. One was a Dutchman called Dolph Lengton who worked for British Petroleum as an area manager and had suggested Lake Eyre in the first place. Another was a thin man with a red beard who worked for Dunlops and had been at Utah when Bluebird crashed. His name was Andrew Mustard. And at Muloorina Campbell met for the first time Elliot Price and Blue Hughes, Elliot's son-in-law.

Campbell's party stayed at Muloorina several days. Hughes

31

knew a spot where it was possible to cross the mud and get onto the surface of the lake, so that surveys were done on foot as well as from the air. Campbell wore his wide-brimmed hat and carried a long tool called an auger to measure the thickness of the salt. He compared the salt of Lake Eyre with the salt he remembered from Utah and was very happy. By the time he was ready to fly back to Adelaide, a large slice of his future had already been decided.

There were difficulties, of course. The lake was inaccessible —thirty-eight miles of spring-breaking bush track to Muloorina and another forty miles to the railhead at Marree, after which there were three changes of gauge along the track to Adelaide. A solid causeway would have to be built across the mud to the hard salt of the lake. And a fifteen-mile track, fifty yards wide, would need to be marked out and smoothed, free of blemishes, flat as a billiard table, somewhere on the lake. At Utah this had been done by pulling heavy drags made of railway lines across the salt. It was a slow business, but there seemed no reason why it should not work here as well. During his fourteen years as a record-breaker, Campbell had grown used to overcoming difficulties.

When he saw Sir Thomas Playford, the veteran Prime Minister of South Australia, he had found things easier than he hoped. The two men got on well together. Once again, as so many times in the past, Campbell described the adventure, the excitement of what he was trying to do, an adventure in which South Australia had a chance to share. If it succeeded —and provided the Bluebird project received its necessary assistance, there was no reason why it should not succeed— Lake Eyre could replace Bonneville and Daytona as the new center of international record-breaking.

That November Campbell gave back the wide-brimmed hat to its owner and returned to London a happy man. Everything, it seemed, was arranged. The South Australian government promised to build a causeway onto the lake and improve the road from Muloorina. The Australian federal government said they would lend troops to provide services and manpower when the record bid began. And Campbell was granted a lease on the lake for one pound (Australian) a year, payable in advance. The lizards had found themselves a new competitor.

"It depends on the lake," Campbell was saying. "If there's a chance in hell of getting her rolling today, darling, I've got to take it. Everyone's been hanging around doing nothing far too long. Morale will simply go if we don't get moving."

It was 6:15 in the morning, and Campbell was walking to the airstrip with his wife, still carrying the blue case he had with him on arrival at Adelaide. Early as it was, dawn was almost over. The greens and mauves and magentas of sunrise were slipping from the horizon, but the air was still sharp and a last star flickered in the west.

"But you never do get ideal conditions. You must just grab what you can while it's there to be grabbed." Campbell's voice echoed back across the flat stillness of the morning, a melancholy statement of fact.

Tonia said nothing in reply. There was nothing she could say. She wore a pink and white scarf around her hair and had a heavy shrouded look. Three black crows loped across the sky as they reached the airplane.

Peter Ahrens, the senior pilot from the plane company, was already waiting in the cockpit, but it seemed taken for granted that Campbell was to handle the controls. Ahrens is a solid, scrupulous man with short blond hair and a thick Swedish neck. He is twenty-eight and his uniform shirts are very white. Campbell went through the plane's check list carefully.

"Flaps. Up and checked."

"Trim tabs. Set and checked."

"Seat belts. Secure."

His voice was emphatic, measured—a good actor's voice. I noticed a scar on his right ear. A dog bit him there when he was eight, and it was badly cut again in the Utah crash.

The port engine coughed, then spluttered to life. The starboard followed. He synchronized them, opened the throttle twice with the brakes still on, set his compass, and we taxied across the drumming red surface of the runway between the mangy dogs and the silent children on old bicycles, past the carcasses of the abandoned trucks, the thickets of rusting beer cans, broken glass, moldering farm implements. Then, gathering speed, we chased the barbed-wire fence toward the wind sock and took off with the sun already risen away on our right in the wide yellow sky.

Tonia was sitting directly behind her husband. She looked as if she had not slept well, and put on her sunglasses when the sun came glittering into the cabin.

Campbell flew with great assurance, taking the Commander up in a wide sweep away from Muloorina until we were heading northeast for the lake. It was a worn, leather-colored landscape we were flying over, an endless overwhelming land.

For a while we followed the Frome River as it faltered across that parched country, splitting, twisting, almost disappearing on its hopeless journey towards the salt lake. Farther north the line of a dingo fence threaded across the wilderness before it, too, disappeared. Then the lake came into view, and as we drew toward it we could see layer upon layer of color swirling off into the distance as the sunlight struck the surface of the salt.

We came in lower, passing the edge of the lake at a few

34

hundred feet, just above the wide rim of mud separating the salt from the land.

To the left, a neat brown line, at right angles to the shore, was the causeway. It was over half a mile long, constructed of rock and earth. Airplanes apart, everything entering or leaving the lake had to cross it.

We circled the camp once. Campbell pointed down to the fresh trucks and cars clustered around the tank shelter where Bluebird was housed.

"Looks as if we're expected," he said, and glanced back, smiling at Tonia. Even that brief spell at the controls of the Commander had done him good. He appeared more assured, more confident than I had seen him and suddenly determined to prove that today was his day and that he and no one else was in command.

"Fine," she said, and took off the sunglasses to smile at him. She has a very beautiful smile—wide, confident, holding nothing back. "It'll be just fine today, darling."

And as if to prove her right, Campbell made a perfect landing with the wheels producing only the faintest crackling on the salt as we touched down.

Leo Villa and his two mechanics had been on the lake since 5:00, preparing the car, and as we climbed from the plane the old man came out to meet us, a solid rather bandy figure with his large, green-lensed spectacles and his oil-stained canvas hat.

"What's it like, Unc?"

"Well, the car's ready when you are, Skipper. Has been for weeks. It's not the car I'm worried about, it's this Goddamn salt." And he stamped with his heel on the salt and pointed to the soft imprint it left behind.

"That's your trouble, Skipper. No guts in it. You can kick a hole in it if you want to. That water from the other night

35

hasn't evaporated as we hoped. It's soaked in and the whole lake's one big bloody sponge."

Villa shares Campbell's habit of overdramatizing things and often repeats his best phrases for effect.

"Just like a bloody sponge, Skipper." As he spoke he stamped again on the salt.

Behind him was the camp. The tank shelter was bigger than it looked from the air—it could have housed a small plane—and around it was all the paraphernalia of a record attempt: oil drums, lengths of piping, a small generating plant, and battered wooden packing cases with "Campbell—Bluebird—Adelaide" stenciled in large black letters on the side.

There was a mobile army workshop, a water trailer, a pair of bright yellow Toyota fueling trucks from Ampol, and several other trucks and cars. But despite all these signs of activity, the whole camp had an air of isolation to it. The sun was beginning to build up its power by now and glared down on the weird landscape of the lake with a brilliance that cut us off completely from any world beyond. Despite the heat there was something arctic about it all.

The light was clear and intense and cruel. Once out in it away from the camp, a man would be swallowed up as certainly as if he lost his way at the North Pole. An individual here would count for very little. Brightness, silence, solitude—this was Lake Eyre. Beyond the camp there was nothing, no landmark, no sign of life—only the bright even circle of the horizon and the glaring sun and the sky above, the palest blue.

It was a silent wilderness. There were no birds to cry, no animals to call. The only sound was the faint whimpering of the wind in the radio mast and the crunch of our own feet as we walked across to the car.

"Well, what d'you think of her?" said Campbell, slapping

Bluebird as a farmer might slap the flank of an expensive heifer.

Inside the dim, green, creosote-smelling cavern of Bluebird's canvas hangar, it was difficult to know what to think. The wheel fairings were off the car, and the mechanics were checking the wheels. By the light of the inspection lamps Bluebird looked incomplete, threatening. It was far bigger than the photographs made it appear. It was also more frightening. Watching the mechanics working on it was like watching the final preparations on some space rocket—the long, carefully polished blue body, the great snout with the air intake at the front, and the tail fin with the glaucous eye of the automatic camera let into the leading edge.

This was the end of the line, the race car driven through its wheels developed to its ultimate, and so specialized that it had only one use—to flash across a carefully prepared mile of salt in the middle of Australia faster than any car had gone before.

The existing record of 394 miles an hour had been set by John Cobb in 1948. Since then Craig Breedlove had reached 412 miles an hour in a jet-propelled car with three wheels. But Breedlove's speed had not been a world record. At that time the Fédération Internationale d'Automobile in Paris was still refusing to recognize jet-propelled vehicles for the speed record. Only a car like Bluebird, driven through the wheels, was eligible.

Villa and his two assistants had been in Australia since February working on the car—cleaning it, stripping it down, polishing it, rebuilding it. After the washout of the previous year it had been stored in a repository in Adelaide.

"It's a brand-new car," said Leo Villa. "Practically unused. Never been run on anything like full power. Used for only a few runs last year and then packed away."

Campbell did not stay long inside the tank shelter looking

at his car. Now that he had seen the salt for himself, Villa's doubts about the wisdom of making a run seemed to be worrying him, too. A group of technicians had gathered outside the hangar waiting for something to happen. Norris was among them.

"Ken, what d'you think of the surface?" asked Campbell.

"Not much, but the water's certainly disappeared quicker than I thought it would. The question is where it's gone to." His voice trailed off. He is a diffident man and dislikes getting into a position where he has to give advice publicly.

Campbell turned away, stamped once or twice on the salt as Villa had done, and looked carefully at the imprint of his boot as if it held the answer to all his troubles.

"Okay, Unc," he called across to Villa at the entrance to the hangar. "You say she's ready. Let's have her out and take a look at her."

It was 7:15. A dozen pairs of hands helped slide the car out. She came slowly, like a big animal from a lair. The sun gleamed on her.

Apart from the faintest of nods to Tonia, Campbell never actually announced his decision to make that first run in Bluebird, but once the car had been brought out it was as if he had no choice. She had to run. And everyone took it for granted now that she would.

Campbell stood for a while talking to Villa. Then the yellow fueling truck was brought up to pump the fourteen gallons for the run into Bluebird's tank. The booster vehicle with the generator to start the turbine followed.

For Campbell the start of each run demanded an elaborate ritual. This was where the small blue case came in. It held the regalia of the record-breaker, the objects without which he would never have dreamed of entering the cockpit. There was the oxygen mask, the blue linen helmet with the headphones for the radio, and the silver jet-pilot's crash helmet, which was

38

given him when he was getting ready for his first attempt v the Bluebird hydroplane by his friend Neville Duke, the pilot. There was a pair of old blue sneakers that he wore in the cockpit, and his two mascots, Whoppit and Whacko. Whoppit, a small bear with a red coat, wore a St. Christopher medal around his neck and had survived the Utah crash with his owner. An indomitable bear, he still traveled in the cockpit. The other bear, Whacko, was like the rest of us, an onlooker. Despite the name, Whacko was a lady, and after every run she had to be reunited with the fearless Whoppit.

The contents of the blue case were Tonia's responsibility. By long practice she knew when they were required. She knew when to hand Campbell the sneakers, and when to give him the silver helmet. It was done in silence. It reminded one of *Ivanhoe* or *Romance of the Rose*. Whoppit went in last.

There was a final check-through with Ken Norris leaning across the cockpit and Campbell testing brakes and radio and controls. Then the cockpit cover was lowered over him, and all you could see was the dim outline of his face with the breathing mask and the silver crown of the crash helmet as he peered out through his one small window. Already he seemed a very long way away.

This was not like an actual race, when there are other cars to compete against and excitement to take the driver's mind off the risks he is taking. This was a cold-blooded, lonely business. All this driver had to compete against was his own weakness and his own fear.

A horn sounded on the booster truck. This was Campbell's own signal to start the turbine. There was a faint pause, then a thin whirring like a high-speed dentist's drill as the compressor turned within the engine. Then came the full roar as the engine came to life. A haze of brown smoke appeared.

Heat flickered from the four big exhaust pipes at the tail, and Bluebird was ready for the first of her trials.

Several of us had a car ready and drove on ahead to watch Bluebird as she passed. We went parallel with the truck and were doing over ninety when the car caught us up. Campbell was handling her gently, and the long blue car passed us with a stately, effortless gliding across the gleaming salt. It could have been flying instead of running on four wheels, and we watched as it went on ahead, picking up speed now, knifing its way up the course, past the big yellow Dunlop flag at the three-mile mark, until it nearly vanished in the glare of the horizon, the tiniest of dots with a cloud of cream-colored salt trailing like a comet's tail behind it.

Villa was watching from the seat of the car. "The salt's too wet to go mucking about like this," he said, shaking his head. "You can't play games on this stuff." But most of us were elated. The sun was shining, the salt was drying, Bluebird was running at last. We stopped the car at the three-mile mark and waited for her to return.

"How long for her to get up to 300?" Wally Parr asked Norris. He had his notebook with him, and the designer gave a cautious reply.

"Some time. Ten days perhaps. Don must get thoroughly at home with the controls, and there's still a lot we need to find out about the old car. We'll want as many runs as we can get from now on." He spoke flatly, as if there were nothing to get worked up about, and he scratched the tip of his nose where it had caught the sun.

Campbell must have turned the car under her own power and made the return run almost immediately, for Bluebird reappeared four or five minutes later. This time she was moving.

"That's well over 200," said Villa, shaking his head again.

The salt cloud behind the car looked larger this time, especially at one point where the water was holding longer than in the rest of the track, and the car seemed to quiver slightly as it struck it. But Bluebird was traveling. That was what mattered. It was so effortless that the gloom of the last few days appeared hysterical and quite ridiculous.

We drove back to the base camp. By the time we reached it Bluebird was at rest outside the tank shelter, and the canopy was open already, sticking up like a marker arrow from the front of the car. Campbell was still in the cockpit, but he had taken his helmet off and was talking to Tonia, who was leaning over the side of the car holding Whacko and the crash helmet.

It was strange how his face had changed. The lines on the forehead had gone. The face itself was fuller. He looked younger, suddenly assertive, and his eyes seemed to have lost that strange, lifeless pallor. He was enjoying the one rightful function of his life at last, and everyone around him knew it.

"We had her all the way up to 220 on the second run on less than twenty-five percent power," he said for the benefit of the people crowding round the cockpit. In the weeks to come I was to recognize the clipped, impersonal voice he reserved for such announcements as these, but at that moment, since everything was so dominated by mood, life seemed suddenly very simple.

A few days at the most. A few days and the car would be up to the record. A few days and the gamble would have paid off. For in a curious way this car had already come to represent something more than the ambition of the man who owned her. All of us were involved in her now. Cut off from the rest of the world, isolated in the middle of this unearthly lake, nothing else had meaning. Failure now would be the failure of us all.

Villa asked suddenly if there were to be any more runs that day, and Campbell nodded and lit himself a cigarette.

41

"Two more, Unc. There and back. Then we must see about something to eat."

It all seemed a matter of routine at the time. All of us helped swing the car around, backing her in a great arc, and when the canopy had closed, the buzzer sounded, and the engine whirred and thundered, the ritual had already become familiar. Most of us stayed behind at the camp this time, and saw the car turn away and head straight onto the glare of the main track. It went swifter than ever. The acceleration of the car was phenomenal, and it was only when it was almost on the horizon that I saw that the cloud of spray behind the car was larger than before.

Carl Noble was sitting up on the top of the army wrecker truck, watching through a pair of binoculars.

"Salt," he shouted down, "only salt. It's the sun makes it look more than it is."

On this run Bluebird took longer to return, and when she did appear she was traveling more slowly than before. Campbell was subdued when he lifted the canopy. "Only 130 that time," he said.

The inspection covers had been lifted off the engine and oil temperatures were being taken.

"Ken," Campbell said to Norris, who was busily noting down the readings in his brown file, "as soon as you've finished I think we'd better take a look at that track."

The meters inside the car give most of the readings Norris needs for his calculations, including engine revolutions, jet pipe temperature, maximum impact on the front suspension, and brake line pressures.

"Don, d'you realize that you recorded 1.8 G. on your suspension that time?" said Norris, looking suddenly perturbed. "That's almost double the force of gravity. You must have hit something one hell of a whack."

42

"Ken, leave that and come up and have a look at the track," said Campbell quietly.

We took the gray Valiant saloon with the muffler sawn off specially for work on the lake. The whole bodywork was now caked in the white- and rust-colored salt, making it look as if it had been delicately iced.

Campbell drove. Although nothing had been said, all the optimism and elation had already gone. So great is Campbell's power of conveying a mood.

We stopped at the four-mile mark. "I think this is the place," he said, speaking for the first time. "Something very odd happened here."

We got out and strolled over to the fifty-yard-wide ribbon of track, which the graders had smoothed until it was like a great highway running to the north. But although it was smooth, the surface was thin, and I remembered what Leo Villa had said. "By midafternoon the heat of the sun will draw the water up through the salt, so that instead of drying in the heat it'll get wetter."

This was what was happening now, and there in the middle of the course were Bluebird's tracks. They ran for a hundred yards each way where the wheels had ploughed three-inch-deep furrows through the slush. Already these furrows had filled with water.

"Well," said Campbell, staring down at one of the furrows and digging at the wet salt crystals with the toe of his boot. "Well?"

Norris started pacing out the length of the ruts. "One hundred and fifty yards," he shouted.

Someone else measured the depth of the water. "Three inches."

"Three inches, Skipper," said Villa. "You've only got four inches clearance on the car. You realize how near you were to scraping your belly on the bloody deck?"

43

"That explains your 1.8 G., Ken," said Campbell. "On the return journey I got my wheels into the ruts I had made on the third run. It was just like getting your wheels in the tramlines at the Elephant and Castle on a wet Saturday night."

By now two more trucks had joined us, and all along the track were melancholy men staring at the ruts, testing the salt with their feet and advancing their own theories of how long it would take to make the track usable again.

"You realize, Skipper, that this is slap up the middle of your course?" Villa said. "You can't do a thing till you've got it cleared up."

"I'll bring the light grader along first thing tomorrow morning," said the large young man who worked with the team preparing the track. "Soon fill up those ruts for you with loose salt. You'll be surprised how quick this salt heals."

But even as he spoke all of us knew it could not be as simple as that. We had left the world of precise difficulties that engineers could do something about. We were up against more mysterious disasters. The surface of Lake Eyre was not something that could be repaired like a torn engine cowling.

"I think," said Campbell, turning back toward the car, "that there are still certain things we need to find out about this course before we try any further runs on it."

CHAPTER FOUR

FROM the air, Campbell's problem was very clear. From six thousand feet in the bright sunlight of the following morning Lake Eyre was immaculate— smooth-surfaced, the salt golden, the horizon never-ending. But when the ailerons dipped and the note of the engine rose and Campbell brought the Aero Commander down to a few hundred feet, turning and banking to the east of the main camp, the salt seemed to change.

It was no longer clear. It varied from one point to another. There were dark gray patches where the water was near the surface, and lighter areas where the salt skin was down to an inch or two. And even where the salt looked thick and hard there was trouble.

"Salt islands everywhere this year," Campbell shouted, shaking his head grimly. "Never seen them like this before."

And for mile after mile they stretched, these strange circular blemishes like a rash across the salt. They were another of the oddities of Lake Eyre. The salt was growing all the time as the water evaporated, and as the crystals built up they would form around anything—the body of a bird or a rabbit, even a leaf or a blade of grass would be enough to start with. It would take some months before the salt island was noticeable, but it would go on growing until it was like the scab of an immense ulcer feeding off the flat surface of the salt. Sometimes it might reach twelve hundred feet in diameter, and its rim could be twelve inches high.

If any fell across Bluebird's track they would need to be leveled. This took time, for they were tough, with a solid core of rock salt hard enough to repel the heaviest grader. When the main track was being prepared Campbell had developed a sort of portable milling machine that actually ground the salt islands away until they were level with the rest of the salt. But a single island could take up to a couple of days to remove, and if we were to find an alternative track there would be no time at all for this. Somehow we had to find a pathway fifteen miles long with hard salt all the way that led *between* the islands. It was like asking for a straight path through the Milky Way.

Another thing we could appreciate from the plane was how well Mustard had chosen the line for the main track. Apparently he had photographed the southern end of the lake from the air and then used the photographs to make a map on which to calculate the one ideal route with the hardest salt and the least number of islands. The only trouble was that the southern end of the lake was now draining straight into the track.

"It looks like it's got to be the old main track or nothing," said Campbell as he headed back toward Muloorina. He was tense and stared straight ahead. His words were meant for no one but himself.

"What do you do if it stays as it was yesterday?" I asked.

"I shudder to think, old sport."

Although I had never met Andrew Mustard, I recognized the angular, red-bearded figure in the light blue overalls of the Bluebird team at once. He was waiting by the runway as we landed. Campbell treated him, I noticed, circumspectly.

"Well, Andy? Good trip back?"

"Thank you, Donald. Yes, I was driving the Humber. Just over seven hours from Adelaide."

"That's fantastic, Andy. You must have nearly killed yourself."

Mustard smiled and put his hands behind his back. "Not quite, Donald. Not quite."

"We had a run yesterday."

"So I've heard."

"Family all right, Andy?"

"Fine, Donald, thank you. Fine."

There was a pause while the two men looked at each other. They were both Scots, but it would have been hard to pick a more total pair of opposites. Mustard, a meditative man, a believer, profoundly serious, with large brown eyes and not an ounce of spare flesh on him, and Campbell, a head shorter and a couple of stone heavier, opinionated, extrovert, a person who acted first and worried about it a long time afterward.

But there was one great bond between them—Bluebird. Both of them were passionately involved in it. Possibly Mustard was the more emotional of the two about the car. It was indisputably Campbell's own car. Mustard was only its reserve driver, and no one was even sure what that meant.

At the moment his chief responsibilities at Lake Eyre were to look after Bluebird's tires and wheels on behalf of the Dunlop Company, which had made them, and to prepare the track. On this last task he had been working like a maniac throughout the previous months, and he had inspired great loyalty from the men who worked with him. Each morning they had been up at 4:30 and slaved on the course through the great heat of the Australian summer.

But Andrew Mustard had never kept it secret that his ambition was to drive Bluebird.

"You know, Ken," he had once said to Norris, "I'd give my right ball to drive that car."

So far the sacrifice had not been demanded of him. As long as Campbell had his way, it never would be. Bluebird's reserve driver had in fact never driven the car, even on a practice run.

"That track of yours, Andrew," said Campbell at last. "It's in a terrible state up around the seven-mile mark."

"That was to be expected after last Friday's rain," replied Mustard in an even voice, which seemed to irritate Campbell.

"We've already had to look for an alternative anyhow," Campbell said sharply.

"I know you have. But I'm not sanguine, Donald. I'm not sanguine."

"Well, what do we do then?"

"You wait, Donald. You wait until it dries. There's nothing else you can do."

Wait we did, throughout the rest of that week, with the tired, addictive boredom of the outback. You could hunt for small scorpions under the stones behind the homestead. You could wade along by the creek observing the geese and ibises and doleful pelicans fishing among the reeds. You could watch the wind-pump and the sunset. You could poison the dingoes with Elliot Price. Whatever you did seemed to bring the record no nearer, and without the record there was no escape.

This waiting was bad for Campbell. It brought out his edginess, his lack of inner resources. He is a man who becomes miserable with nothing to do. He talked of flying up toward Alice Springs for the day but nothing came of it, and he spent his mornings playing a form of solitaire called Russian boule and his afternoons cleaning his guns—a .22 Winchester and a pair of very smart Spanish .32 automatics bought in Adelaide.

48

A change had come over him in the last few days. Whatever hopes he had had of a quick, exciting run at the record had gone completely. He knew how little chance of success there was, and he was convinced that something was against him. There was a touch of hopelessness about the way he pottered around the house in his blue blazer, waiting with dull persistence for the chance he needed.

It was a bad time for Tonia, too. Muloorina was not for her, and she hated the boredom of waiting.

"They're always the same, these record bids," she said, "always straightforward until we get there. But he's worried this time—deep down he's really worried, and there's nothing I can do for him. I'd like to tell him to pack it up, but that's one thing he must never suspect. You see, I have to be his pal and I have to humor him. I mustn't nag or worry or have any doubts about what he's doing as any ordinary wife would. He's had two wives already and the record business finished them. So I must be different."

Only once, while we were waiting, did Campbell show any sign of the bitterness he was feeling. It was on Friday night; he was sitting opposite me in Elliot Price's large green armchair beneath the three china sea gulls flying along the wall on their eternal journey toward the mantelpiece.

"It should be all right," he said. "That bloody main track should be all right. Andrew Mustard has spent five thousand pounds of my money preparing it."

He puffed at his pipe and looked suddenly old and rather lost, hunched as he was in his chair.

"Still, we'll know the truth tomorrow. I'm giving it a couple of runs at 8:00 A.M. That should tell us whether we're properly in the stuff."

Saturday dawned, a clear golden morning such as you get only in the Australian outback in the early winter, and as we flew out to the lake it seemed to welcome us—a gala lake,

49

clear and cold, shell-pink and lilac. That morning it had the perfection of something just created.

There were even a few spectators waiting this time as the plane landed, and some relatives of Elliot Price, who had driven across in a cream-colored Ford Zephyr.

The film people were out in strength, the cameramen setting up their tripods for a last-minute interview with Campbell before the run. Isolated as we had been in the desert with this anxious man, we had forgotten that the world outside was interested in him, too.

There was no chance of a record yet, no chance even of any great speed. But Bluebird is dangerous enough to be exciting whenever she runs, and beneath the excitement a few of us knew the truth. The main track was having its final trial. If it failed this morning we would know that it was useless, and that Campbell's chances of getting the record were over.

But all this was hidden behind a great show of efficiency preceding the run. Everyone was caught up in it. Andrew Mustard's men on the track were wearing new, immaculate white overalls. The name "Andrew Mustard Limited" was printed in red script diagonally across the back, and underneath, in smaller letters, "Lake Eyre, 1964."

Mustard was nervous. Whether he liked it or not, his reputation depended on what happened to the car seven miles up on the track. He seemed preoccupied and spoke to no one except to give an occasional order to his men.

But quite apart from Mustard's team, all Campbell's party was out in force: Leo Villa with his sunglasses, Ken Norris in his maroon shirt, his brown folder under his arm, and the specialist engineers from the different companies associated with Campbell on the record bid—Scrimshire of Motor Panels, Sir Alfred Owen's firm, which had actually built Bluebird, Reaks of Smith's Instruments, with his large mustache, and

Carl Noble of Electro-Hydraulics in an old pair of Bluebird team overalls, which he had worn at Utah in 1960.

"Okay. Roll her out," shouted Campbell, and all of us went to help.

It was still early, not 8:00 yet, but the light was diamond hard and shone brilliantly on the clean-cut lines of the car.

Campbell stood on his own, looking lost and forgotten as he always did before a run. There was nothing for him to do until the moment when he had to risk his life, and none of us could help him. I found myself near him and was curiously embarrassed that he was risking his neck and I was not. It was a barrier between us. All I could think of saying was how beautiful the car was.

He nodded. "Except for those damn great wheels," he said. "You know how big they are. Fifty-two inches in diameter. Just think how much better she would look with smaller wheels. Ken did a beautiful job fitting them into the car, but I've always thought they ruin the look of the thing."

He paused and lit himself a cigarette. "It was those wheels that nearly did for me in Utah. Once you get into a spin with wheels that size, you've had it."

For a moment it was as if he were talking to himself. Then he realized he had said too much, and walked off without another word to join Tonia.

She always managed to be unflustered, slightly casual with him before a run—very much the pal now, no sign of the worried wife. It was an admirable performance. She was wearing black and white checked slacks and a silk blouse, and her hair was tied with a white ribbon. As far as the newspapers were concerned she was simply "Tonia Bern, cabaret singer," but she was more than that. She was a woman of character. She had common sense, and she was practical and clever enough to keep her fears to herself.

They talked for a few minutes. Then she gave him his

51

mascot and his helmet and his oxygen mask. He slid himself onto the side of the cockpit, then she took his boots and handed him the blue sneakers. The operating-theater routine of starting up began as Campbell and Norris started their last check.

"Master switch—On."

"Accelerometer—On."

"Check breathing air."

"Gearbox pumps—pressures correct."

Campbell's voice was muffled now, coming from deep within the car, and although the cockpit cover was still open, it was already the voice of someone about to be cast off—a diver before his helmet is bolted down, a spaceman before communications cease.

The lid went down. The buzzer sounded again as it had sounded four days before. Once again the engine whirred, then roared to life, and the turbine lashed out with its power, sending the smoke and the heat freckling across the salt.

As Bluebird moved off, Wally Parr was busily taking photographs with a small camera of his own. He seemed uncomfortable to be caught doing anything so unprofessional. "For the family album," he said. "Thought it worth taking a few happy snaps. After all, she's the last of these things we're likely to see. By the way," he added, "has he been talking to you too about the Utah crash? It's odd. You'd think he'd want to forget a thing like that."

The brilliance of the light on the lake foreshortened every distance, and the heat haze was so intense that by 11:00 the horizon came down to about a mile. At two hundred yards a car appeared to float in midair. At a quarter of a mile a tent began to form a quavering mirror image beneath it. And at a mile it would be swallowed up in the glare where the lake surface and the sky joined in a permanent arc of light.

One moment the car was in front of you in that hard white

light that permitted no shadows and made it seem the most tangible thing in the world. Then, as the turbine roared, the salt spurted from the wheels, the sun flashed on the great tail, and Bluebird was away, swifter than any rocket. This was not a car being driven. It was a launching into outer space, a conjuring trick where speed and light and silence and distance were all there to deceive the senses.

Campbell was the only person for whom Bluebird's journey could have any reality. For him, in his cockpit, there was the flashing past of the big colored canvas markers at each mile, and the wide blue dye line running up the center of the track for him to steer by. For the four or five minutes of a run he had his dials to watch, the rate of acceleration to take care of, and the certainty that if anything did go wrong it would all be over before he could do very much about it. At three hundred miles an hour in the half second between his senses noticing, his mind reacting, his arm or leg moving, and the controls functioning, the car would have traveled through two hundred and twenty feet. A spin, a skid, a sudden loss of control, and the moment in Utah which he seemed unable to forget would be repeating itself somewhere up there amid the glare and the mirages of the lake.

That morning there was a long wait after Bluebird had roared off into the distance, and when the car finally reappeared it came so slowly that we knew at once something was wrong. Campbell slid the car to a halt, lifted the cockpit cover, and sat there, silent and slightly dazed.

"Well, Skipper?" said Villa at last.

"It's no good," said Campbell, handing him the crash helmet. "No good at all. I put on less than twenty-five percent power and the wheels went right through the surface just beyond the seven-mile mark. Exactly the same as the other day. It's not going to dry out, and there's no question of further runs on it, Unc. You couldn't ride a bicycle safely on it at the moment."

So it was all over. He sat there in the cockpit and no one spoke because there was nothing to say, but Tonia had the sense to get his boots for him and tell him there was coffee in the hangar and it was getting cold.

He clambered out then. The news photographers took the pictures they needed to go with their reports on Campbell calling off an attempt for the second year running. The newsreel cameraman stopped him and said, "Hold it, Donald. Just a moment, if you would. We'd like a good shot of you looking depressed."

Campbell smiled wearily, and all he said was, "I suppose I must look as I feel."

He walked away, not toward the hangar but to the gray Valiant. Once in the car, sitting at the wheel, his calm began to crack.

"Damn place. Filthy damn place," he said under his breath, and slammed his foot on the accelerator. The wheels spun on the salt and we jerked forward down the service road. Suddenly he swung straight onto the middle of the main track, and raced down it at ninety, following the wheel marks Bluebird had left twenty minutes before.

"No need to worry about this any more." He was beginning to shout now.

"Fifteen miles of uselessness. Six months' work. I don't know how many thousand pounds' worth of machinery, and you end up with precisely nothing."

We stopped, and all trooped silently from the car at a point where the ruts were very deep. There was no point in Ken Norris pacing them out this time or measuring them. They seared into the track from one end to the other. The salt everywhere was wet and crumbling.

For a while Campbell looked down at the track, his face

gray in the bright sun and the tears running down his cheeks. The sunlight glinted on the neat row of salt crystals the wheels had banked on each side of the ruts. The sky was very blue.

He had waited nine years for this moment, and now there was nothing to be said and nothing to be done except get back into the car and drive home.

CHAPTER FIVE

"AND now all you South Australians, the time is 6:15 and this is the news from ABC read by Ralph Binns. On Lake Eyre today British record-breaker Donald Campbell had two trial runs on his specially prepared track and found the surface of the salt so softened after recent rains that he was unable to get above 180 miles an hour. Campbell said afterward that he thought things were hopeless, and he is expected to postpone his bid for the world land speed record until September."

So that was that.

"Quite right, too," said Elliot Price, leaning forward to turn off the radio. "He'll kill himself if he goes on here. Come September the lake'll be dried out real proper, but you can't expect the man to go ahead with the salt in the state it is now."

"That's the end, then," said Wally Parr. "He can't postpone it again. This was his last chance, and if he leaves now he might as well give Bluebird to the Science Museum and pack up for good."

"I don't see why," Elliot said. "September'd be fine. The car's all right and the man's all right. It's just a case of waiting and having trust in Donald to pull it off when the lake's in better shape."

But although nobody argued with the old man, most of us

knew that Parr was probably right. A record-breaker is good for only a certain number of failures, and Campbell had exceeded his quota. There would not be the money or the enthusiasm or the time or the energy for another go in September. The record had to be now or never.

The news of the postponement spread quickly and produced a strange mood of light-heartedness within the camp. This was not from any particular animosity against Campbell. At this point he was still popular enough. It was simply that people had had enough of Muloorina and enough waiting around doing nothing. It was a luxury to have a decision at last. Whatever the disappointment for Campbell, it was impossible not to be glad it was over. Because of this there was a touch of guilt behind the sympathy we showed him when he appeared for dinner that evening. And as it turned out, the dinner was especially good.

"We don't want any food left behind this time," Tonia had said as she drove back that afternoon from the lake. "Last year we had to pull out in such a hurry after the rains came that we had to leave behind fifty pounds' worth of provisions."

So that night we were eating what would otherwise have been wasted, but the meal had something of a celebration about it all the same. There was asparagus soup—good, thick, Belgian soup with small drops of fat glistening on the surface, and large chunks of canned asparagus added. And there was steak and broad beans and boiled potatoes and fried potatoes, and most of us ate with a sort of weary relief that the whole thing was over. We were hungry after the day on the lake, and by eating well and asking for second helpings of the tough, metallic-tasting rump meat that was the best the cattle could make out of this dead, gray land, we were showing ourselves that there was more to life than Lake Eyre.

Campbell sat at the head of the table as usual, and to start with we attempted to avoid his eye, for it was wrong to be

"Well, Andy," said Campbell. "It looks like one of those things, doesn't it."

After dinner that night there was another meeting of the entire team up in the old shearers' quarters, and everyone was there to hear Campbell speak his own epitaph.

"It's going to be interesting to hear how he phrases it," Wally Parr said, taking out his notebook as Campbell arrived. "And I want to hear what our friend Mustard has to say for himself."

"Good evening, gentlemen," Campbell said. He stood for a few seconds waiting for the conversation to die away, a solid, suddenly impassive figure, puffing at what was left of his cigar. In the half hour since dinner he had changed yet again. He was tense now and deadly serious. He was standing almost directly beneath the light that showed up the small bald patch at the back of his head. The room became suddenly very silent.

"Gentlemen. There was a report on the radio tonight that I am postponing the attempt until September. I have no idea how such a report reached the Australian Broadcasting Corporation, but I would like to say here and now that it is totally and utterly incorrect. Nothing is being postponed. Today was a disappointment. A bitter disappointment. But nothing, I repeat nothing, is being postponed."

He paused, and the smoke from his cigar swirled up against the light. The only sound in the room was the noise of Parr's pencil as he took down the statement for the benefit of next morning's papers.

"The other day, fearing this might happen, several of us made an aerial reconnaissance to look for a possible alternative to the present main track. We saw what looked like a possible area to the east. It is clear after this morning's run

60

that the present main track is not going to be in a condition to take Bluebird during the foreseeable future, so we must find somewhere that will. The search will commence tomorrow morning at first light. I will fly in the Aero Commander, and I will need as much support as I can have from the ground. The procedure will be as follows. I will select what looks like a possible route from the air. I will signal by dipping the wings of the plane and the cars can follow. We will need your cooperation in this, gentlemen, and I would be grateful for as many as possible of you with your cars on the lake tomorrow morning.

"I need hardly add that time is of the essence in this entire operation. The situation is desperate. It need not be impossible. Are there any questions?"

Parr asked about arrangements for track preparation once a new course was found. "If the present main track took six months to prepare, how long will it be before you are ready to run even if you do find the sort of area you need?"

"That, Wally, is a problem we must meet when we come to it. I know how much time and effort the present main track cost. It also took a great deal of my money. I was never entirely convinced that the track should have been prepared that far in advance of the record attempt."

If Mustard had been going to speak, this was his cue. He was sitting on one of the iron bedsteads, wearing a blue blazer and a white shirt with a floppy collar and a blue silk club tie. But he kept silent.

"Right, gentlemen," said Campbell. "Lake Eyre, at 7:00 tomorrow morning."

If it had not been for the meal and the cigars and the story about the German general, it is just possible that he might not have got away with it. Before we went to dinner that night most of us had been convinced that there was no hope

61

and were anxious to be off. But things were different now. He had established contact with us over dinner. We had eaten with him and drunk his whisky and laughed at his stories, and if he wanted to go on looking for another track there was not a great deal we could do about it.

The journey to the lake was nearly thirty miles, and on that road it took most drivers three quarters of an hour as they cornered and skidded across the ruts and potholes and drifts of stifling red bull-dust. The trek had begun at sunrise with every car available—the official Humber with "Bluebird Project, Lake Eyre 1964" in heavy white lettering on the side, the hired cream-colored Fords, the big gray Valiants, the battered Land Rover—all jolting down the track from the homestead as the sun came up, past the leafless coolibahs, bone white above the creek, past the wattle thickets with the flocks of gray and red parakeets, past the gum trees with the mud nests of the epicoma caterpillars swinging from the branches like heavy gray udders.

Ahead lay a fantastic landscape. The cars were trailing great streamers of dust, and the land each side was as flat and as empty as if it had been scraped with an immense steel ruler. Most wildlife had been destroyed. Kangaroos were a rarity by day, although sometimes in the distance you could see a pair of emus racing away as you approached.

A few miles from the lake the landscape changed, and where the road built by the army ran alongside the edge of the lake it was like approaching the shores of the Dead Sea. On the right were strange formations of sandstone eroded by the wind until they could have been the ruined fortress walls of some forgotten civilization. To the left of the road were the first layers of the mud surrounding the lake, mud that had cracked and wrinkled and corrugated and set into a hundred different textures, gray and red mud, with here and there the faintest silvering of salt.

We bumped our way over the causeway. The number of vehicles across it had already ploughed up the far end, and the lake itself was more than ever like a lake of ice, with the salt churning up like snow crystals.

At the base camp Villa and the mechanics were working away at the car again. However slender the chance now that Bluebird could ever run, it was typical of him to keep to perfection.

Campbell was there, too, a keen, decisive Campbell with large notebook and binoculars and several compasses. He also had the knapsack he always carried in rough country, a habit he had picked up from his father. It contained string, knife, brandy, water bottle, and a revolver that fired small shot in case of snakes.

"Now you know what we want," he said. "Smooth, hard salt, devoid of salt islands." And when he had issued the compasses, he gave us bearings to follow and told us that wherever we found anything we should halt the car and wait until the plane came over.

He has a great knack of arranging plans, organizing expeditions, giving orders. He once told me that his ambition as a boy was to become an army officer. The OTC was one of the few things he had really enjoyed at school at Uppingham, and when we had all received our instructions and were ready to go, there was a distinct air of a school field day about it all.

"Don't forget," shouted Campbell, giving us one last piece of advice, "if you get lost stick with the car. We'll soon spot you from the air, but once you go wandering off on your own, there's a chance we won't see you again."

One by one the cars fanned out eastward, trying to find what no one except Campbell believed could be found—a clear stretch of salt, fourteen miles long, hard enough to bear not just the weight of Bluebird, but the force of its great wheels as they kicked with all the power of that five thousand horsepower engine at four hundred miles an hour.

As soon as we were away from the camp, Lake Eyre took over. At the base camp, as Campbell gave his orders in that precise young army officer's voice of his, it had all seemed straightforward. But less than ten minutes later, as I continued on my course of two hundred ninety degrees east, I realized that I was utterly lost. The trouble was the very brightness of the lake. In this gleaming white world there was not a landmark to set a compass by, and all you could do was to drive on, trying to follow your senses, but knowing all the time that you were veering constantly from one way to the other. On their own the senses are deceptive, and all the time mirages sprang up above the salt islands, looking like cars or tents or groups of people, only to vanish as you got closer.

Once I passed a duck that must have been blown onto the lake. It rose weakly as the car approached, flew a few yards, and then flopped onto the wet salt again. By midday the sun would have finished it off. Within a few weeks it would be starting a salt island of its own.

Even from the air I had not realized how much the surface of the salt varied. At one point it would be so wet that water swished and spurted from the wheels and the car left deep runnels behind it. Half a mile on, I would be threading my way between small, tightly packed salt islands. A little later there were small tufts to the salt, an inch or so high, that crunched like glass beneath the wheels. And every so often came the salt Campbell needed if he was to get his record—hard, smooth, impermeable salt, with a surface like perfectly laid concrete. There would be a patch, then just as it seemed we had what we needed, the wheels struck the wet again.

I had been driving like this for more than half an hour

64

when I spotted the small blue and white plane circling away to the left, and although I lost sight of it, it gave me the direction I needed, and I drove over. It is surprising how fast a car can travel on this salt when it has to. But Campbell had already landed by the time I got there.

The airplane was on one of the hard patches of salt, and Campbell was talking to Ken Norris, who had driven one of the other cars. He looked excited, more decisive and clear-cut than ever. He had put on a red and white ascot and was trying to pick a hole in the salt with the end of his clasp knife.

"Well, old boy, if it's anywhere it's here," he said. "It's pretty rough in places, but it runs for eight miles before it gets soft again and it's free of salt islands."

"But eight miles?" I said. "What use is that?"

"Well, it's a start, for heaven's sake. There's a lot we can do with eight miles."

"But you can't get the record with that length."

"At least I can get the car moving. That will be something, and afterward you never know. There may be a chance of squeezing another mile or two at each end when the salt has dried out a bit."

"But you need fourteen miles of flat hard salt."

"Can't be too choosey now. If I have to try and make do with less, I'm afraid it'll be just too bad."

And by now I had been on Lake Eyre long enough to know what that would mean. Neither a yes nor a no. Just the slenderest of chances, the most tantalizing of possibilities that the lake was offering now to keep us here. Already I thought of the lake as a person—cunning, beautiful, malignant, with moods that were always changing and an intelligence that was going to extract the greatest pleasure out of tormenting Campbell before it finally destroyed him.

CHAPTER SIX

FROM where Campbell was standing at the eastern end of his new track, the small black outline of the Land Rover seemed scarcely to move and the silence of the lake was so total that while it was still a long way off we could hear the noise of the engine and the strangely lulling, crunching sound of the big steel drag ironing down the roughness of the salt.

"It's a slow business, Andy," said Campbell.

"It is indeed," Mustard replied.

Slowly the Land Rover advanced toward us. It began to look like some hard-shelled insect.

"Is it nearly done now?" Campbell asked.

"It's getting as good as we can reasonably hope for. If we smooth it away much further we're likely to destroy the hardest part of the surface and there's water only a few inches down."

This was the fifth day of work on the new track, and while the rest of the camp had been waiting back at Muloorina the two Land Rovers had been out on the empty lake from dawn until dusk plying their way backward and forward along the eight miles of the new course. They never exceeded five miles an hour. Several times the welded steel joints between the steel rails of the drags had come apart and precious hours were lost while they were laboriously repaired. On Sunday rain was forecast, and although it never fell a belt of felt-gray raincloud hung over the west of the lake for the next couple of days.

But now on Wednesday, May 13th, the work was nearly done. The clouds had gone. It looked as if Bluebird would soon have a chance to run again. Campbell seemed cheerful, almost excited this morning.

"They seem to have done a great job, your chaps, Andy—a great job."

He kicked the salt with his heel and nodded approvingly when he saw that it made scarcely an impression. "If the rest of the track is as good as this, I think we'll really be getting somewhere."

Mustard was wearing white overalls and canvas shoes. He looked tall and angular beside the squatter, more solid figure of Campbell. The wind ruffled the hair away from the smooth bald dome above his forehead. His eyes were hidden behind rimless sunglasses, and it was hard to see how he was reacting to Campbell's praise.

"Well, Donald, I would suggest that we don't overlook the fact that this end, the northern extremity of the course, possesses much the most satisfactory surface." His diction was precise, professorial, his thought guarded. "Farther south it begins to deteriorate a fraction, but on the whole I think you should find the course will meet your minimal requirements."

"You do, do you. Well, I think we should all have a quick look. Is that all right with you, gentlemen?"

"Fine, Skipper. Quite agree," said Leo Villa.

"Yes," said Ken Norris, nodding and biting his lower lip. Neither of them showed great enthusiasm for the new course, but if Campbell was happy that was something.

"Have you carried out adhesion tests on the new track yet?" Norris asked Mustard as we climbed into the gray Valiant saloon.

"But naturally, Kenneth. Naturally. Although I wouldn't attach too much credence to them at this stage of the game. Since the last rains the surface of the lake seems to be changing from one hour to the next. It is my considered opinion that all runs should take place as soon after first light as humanly possible. The effect of the sun is to draw the water toward the surface of the salt, making the lake progressively softer toward midday."

Mustard gained confidence as he spoke. He relishes being an expert, and however much of a knock his reputation may have taken over the failure of the old main track, the completion of this new one had worked wonders for his morale.

Campbell drove the Humber. He was wearing his red and white checked neck scarf and had started chewing spearmint gum. All his attention was on the track.

This new track of his lay several miles to the east of the old main course, and at right angles to it. The only chance of extending it was to the west, but if this was done it would mean crossing the waterlogged surface of the old track at about the third-mile mark.

"Okay, everyone. Hold very tight," Campbell shouted suddenly, and before we knew what was happening he had slammed on the brakes and locked the wheels. The Humber skidded to a halt.

Leo Villa pushed his spectacles back from the end of his nose.

"Phew, Skipper. What's the idea?"

"A little test, Leo. Now let's get out and measure the length of the skid marks. That ought to give us a rough guide to the adhesion value of the salt. Don't you think so, Ken?"

"Yes, I think we can work something out from that. What speed were we doing when you locked the brakes?"

"Thirty exactly."

"Let's have a look at the skid marks then."

We were about two miles from the start of the track and the salt was in good condition here. Even so, the top layer of the salt was damp, and when we measured out the skid marks with the old leather-cased surveyor's tape Campbell kept in his knapsack we found that it had taken the Humber thirty-five yards to stop.

"What d'you think of that, Ken?" Campbell asked sharply. "Is it good enough for us?"

"Looks a bit dodgy to me, Don, but I'd like a few more figures to go on. D'you think you could repeat the performance at intervals along the track?"

Norris squatted uncomfortably with the large brown folder open on his knees.

"Don't forget, Donald," said Mustard, looking at his watch, "the time is now 11:25. The lake is approaching its wettest period of the day. At first light you would get a better reading."

"Point taken, Andy. But let's do as Ken suggests. It'll give us something to go on."

So we spent the remaining eight miles accelerating, skidding, and measuring. Ken Norris recorded the results in his folder without comment.

"Well," said Campbell when we had reached the western end of the track. "It's a course. I'll say that for it."

He spat out his chewing gum, lit a cigarette, and blew the smoke thoughtfully between pursed lips.

"It still seems very rough, Andy, and this end is pretty wet. Are you sure you can't get it any smoother?"

"I could, Donald, but it would mean destroying the hardest part of the salt. The more we smooth it the wetter it gets."

"Okay, Andy. We'll have to see what Ken's figures have to tell us. And thank your chaps for me. I think they've worked wonders."

Campbell drove back to the base camp with Villa and

Norris, leaving Mustard, who wanted to check the laying of the blue dye line that marked the center of the course.

Back in the hangar, Campbell turned to Villa and said, "Well, Unc, it looks like tomorrow morning, first thing. The sooner we get started the better. Will Bluebird be ready to roll at 7:00?"

"She's ready to go now if you want her. But, Skipper, I don't like that bloody track. The car wasn't designed for a surface like that, and frankly I don't see the point of risking it just for the sake of a run."

There were corned beef sandwiches left behind by the mechanics, and the three men made themselves comfortable on the duckboards beside the jacked-up body of the car. As they munched the thick, slightly stale bread, they conducted their private inquest on the new track. The main problem, of course, was the adhesion. On a dry, hard surface such as concrete, the wheels of a car like Bluebird slip minimally and the thrust remains strong. But on a wet surface like the salt the wheels spin, lessening the thrust and, at speed, sometimes sending the car out of control.

Now Campbell looked at Norris and said, "What about those adhesion figures of yours, Ken? Using the Valiant like that was a pretty rough-and-ready method, but it ought to give us some inkling of the real hazards of the course."

Norris had his brown folder open in front of him and held a sandwich in his left hand, a pen in his right.

"Not very bright, Don. In fact," he took a bite of the sandwich, "you could say very dim. The minimum adhesion factor we require for safety is .7. The best we seem to have got this morning was just over .5, and that was at the beginning of the track. Farther on we seem to have been down to .45. Of course, Andrew may be right. It may be a lot better before the sun heats it up, and these figures are pretty rough. But I can't say it's very good, particularly on a track this length where you'll have to accelerate fast. If you had twelve or fourteen miles it might be different, but you've only eight. You'll have to watch for those wheels spinning every inch of the way."

"That's what I mean, Skipper," said Villa quickly. "Try and extend your course and then have a go, but on this new track it's murder. And we know what happens when adhesion goes and Bluebird's wheels start spinning."

There was a long silence. "Unc," Campbell said at last, "if you look in that big cardboard box over there by your right foot I think you'll find a jar of mustard pickle. I would be very grateful if you would dig it out for me. These sandwiches could do with something to liven them up."

"My father?" said Campbell. "Obviously he has been the most important single influence on my life, and you could come up with some very fancy Freudian theories to explain what I'm up to at Lake Eyre."

Norris and Villa still had work to do on the car and had decided to stay on. Campbell and I drove back together in the Morris 1100.

"You must remember that I grew up in the shadow of the great man. He was a formidable person to have as a father. He was tough. Dynamic. Quite ruthless at getting anything he really wanted."

From the point where we left the shores of the lake, the road deteriorated into a series of bends and gullies often covered in drifts of yielding red dust. But he handled each hazard with a sort of preoccupied neatness. The speed never dropped below seventy.

"Of course he had great charm, too, a kind of boyish vitality and enthusiasm for anything he took on. In some ways he never stopped being a schoolboy. He liked the things boys like—cars, airplanes, gadgets of all sorts. You've heard all

71

about his treasure hunting. In 1926, you know, he went off in search of Spanish treasure on Cocos Island in the Pacific. Went with his old friend Kennelm Lee Guiness, the man the KLG spark plug was named after. The treasure was there, all right. They located the position according to the old charts, but couldn't reach it. The Marquis of Bristol later discovered a cave but the roof had fallen in and the actual treasure was under the sea. It's always been a great dream of mine to go back with drills and diving apparatus and have a crack at finding the old man's treasure. I'd get a great kick out of that.

"He used to take me poaching with him sometimes, too, when I was a kid. He was good for anything with a bit of adventure in it."

We had reached a long straight stretch of track. Campbell wound down his window and lit a cigarette as he drove.

"For me, childhood was like growing up with an extraordinarily successful elder brother in the house. I think I reacted very much as younger brothers are supposed to in such circumstances. In some ways it held me back, made me unsure of myself. You remember asking me the other day why I never thought of going in for a record while Father was alive. Well, there was no question of it. In our family Father was the one who got the records.

"I used to kick hard against the old man, too. We fought. For crying out loud, we fought. He was such a character that you had to fight him or else go under completely.

"To make it worse, while I was trying hard to be like him—I aped him at one period, even tried to brush my hair the way he did—he was just as determined to turn me into everything he was not. 'You know what your father would have been if he'd been born two hundred years earlier?' he used to say. 'A pirate, boy. A pirate and a jolly good one, too.'

"But he didn't want me to be a pirate. He wanted me to be

something respectable in the City. He tried very hard. I'll say that for Father, he tried.

"He was mean, too—very tight about money. In 1925, for instance, old Leo had just got back to England after they'd set the new 300 miles an hour land speed record and shoved in his expenses for the journey. Don't forget that in those days Leo was earning a few pounds a week and working like a Trojan for it. All the same, Father went through those expenses with a fine-tooth comb and saw an entry for oysters on Leo's celebration dinner. Out they came. 'Why should I pay for oysters?' he said."

By now we were at the bleak center part of the journey, with the plain all round flat and limitless. He increased the speed and fell silent.

"And how did this strange relationship with your father affect you in the end?" I asked.

"I wouldn't know. That's for other people to say. I'm still trying to find the answers for myself."

Campbell was cheerful that night at dinner, and as always his good humor was infectious. There was leek soup and cottage pie and carrots, and Elliot Price told the story of how his stomach fell through his diaphragm one afternoon when he was standing on his head to amuse his youngest grandchild.

"You've no idea of the pain, Don. Terrible. Terrible it was. If it hadn't been for Mother and the family I'd have asked the doctor to finish me off once and for all."

"But what happened, Elliot? How did your guts land back in the right place?" asked Campbell.

"Well, Don. It's quite a story. Took me down to Adelaide they did. X-rayed me. Brought all the specialists in. Prodded me, shook me around, and then told me that when I stood on

73

my head the weight of my guts had split my diaphragm and wedged 'em up into my chest.

" 'What you going to do about it?' I asked 'em. 'I'm in agony.'

" 'Well, Mr. Price,' they said, 'we can operate but you'll only have a fifty-fifty chance of pulling through!'

" 'Fifty-fifty, doctor,' I said. 'That's no good to me. If that's the best hope you can give me, I'm off.'

"So back to Muloorina I come. Still in agony. Terrible agony. But at least I'm alive, you understand. Mother looks after me."

"But Elliot," said Campbell, lighting a cigar, "you still haven't told us how you got all those guts of yours back in the right place."

"Give me time, Donald, give me time. What happens is as follows. For six months I'm in bed. The agony goes on. Can't keep any food down. I'm at the end of my tether. Then one night, after 11:00 it is, the policeman from over Marree arrives here, knocks on the door and shouts 'Elliot. We needs help quick. There's bastard sheep-stealers on your land.'

" 'Bastard sheep-stealers,' I said. 'The bastards.'

" 'Yes,' he shouts. 'They're after your bastard sheep. What're you going to do about it, Elliot?'

" 'I'm coming with you, Constable,' I says.

" 'What, in your condition?'

" 'Yes, in my condition. I've had enough of this lying in bed in agony. If I've got to go I'll go now, but so help me, I'll get those bastard sheep-stealers first.'

"So I take my gun and get in beside him in his big Dodge truck and away we go, driving like mad after these sheep-stealers. It's black as pitch and the headlights aren't much good.

"Then suddenly it's like a flash of lightning hitting me, a

74

great flash of pain that goes right through me, and I scream out with it.

" 'Elliot,' he says, shocked-like. 'Are you all right? We've bumped into a great hole in the track.'

" 'All right?' I says. 'I'm finished. I'm going to die. Just leave me there by the foot of that tree and then get them bastard sheep-stealers. That'll let me die happy.'

"So he lays me down, gentle-like, by the tree. And off he goes. And somehow I don't die. I start feeling better instead. And an hour later when the Constable arrives back with the two bastard sheep-stealers expecting to be finding my corpse at the foot of the tree, he sees me standing on my own two feet and as well as I am today.

"You see," said the old man, leaning back in his chair and grinning, "it was the jolt that done it. Jolted my guts back down to their rightful place again. And I never had trouble with them since."

"But what did the doctors say when they saw you?" asked Campbell.

"Well, you know what doctors are, Donald. They don't believe anything they don't want to. But I always tell people that story because I reckon there's a moral to it."

"Perhaps there is, Elliot," said Campbell smiling and looking straight at him with those pale eyes of his. "Perhaps it means that people of our age shouldn't go standing on our heads to amuse the children."

Now that Campbell had decided to try out his new track, Tonia had a new worry, and after dinner she had a quiet word with Leo Villa. He had always been a particular ally of hers, and she knew there were things Campbell would confide in him that he would never dream of telling her.

"Leo, it's really all right for tomorrow, isn't it?"

"All right? Lord, yes. Perfectly straightforward. The Skipper's just doing a routine run to test out his new track."

"Are you *sure* that's all he's going to do?" she said.

"Of course that's all he'll do. What else do you think could happen?"

"I don't know. Perhaps it's silly of me, Leo, but I got the feeling this afternoon that somehow Donald's attitude to the car was changing. He seemed to have a sort of fever for it. You know how he used to get like that sometimes with the boat, and how he was just before the crash at Utah."

Villa looked at her quickly. "There's nothing like that. I know him and I'd tell you if there was. All he's doing tomorrow is a slow run to try out the track."

He must have realized then that he was being too emphatic. "Now, Tonia," he said. "It's no good worrying about the Skipper. He knows what he's up to. Tomorrow will be all right."

Campbell's plane, blue and white, trim as ever, touched down on the lake at 7:55 the next morning, and we watched him step out of the small rectangular door beneath the wing, wave a brisk good-morning to Leo Villa, and then help down Tonia, who handed him the ever-present blue leather bag. He looked lively enough.

Wally Parr was standing beside me. "You don't really think he wants to kill himself?" he asked.

"Not for a moment," I said. "If there's anyone who really enjoys life, it's Donald. And he is very cautious. If he were the suicidal type he'd have died years ago."

"Yes, I suppose so," said Parr. "We'd better take our pictures before he gets into Bluebird." And both of us consulted light meters and set cameras. The ritual of these photographs was one of the more macabre touches of record-breaking.

People took them all the time because they always felt it necessary to have just one last picture of him in case anything happened.

Through the view finder Campbell made a good picture as he stood by the car talking to Ken Norris with the white salt and the sapphire blue of the car as a background. His profile is quite different from his full face. He looks stronger, more commanding, and as I focused the camera on him the slightly beaked nose, the hard jaw line, the sudden wrinkles as he screwed his eyes against the sun reminded me of old photographs of his father from the early Thirties.

"But the atmosphere of this morning's run is all wrong," Parr continued as the shutter of his camera clicked. "Things must be very desperate with him now. I just don't see what he can do with this eight-mile track, but he seems quite excited by it. Perhaps the old death wish is stronger than you think."

Certainly Campbell was impatient to be off, and the urgency of the occasion communicated itself to everyone. Andrew Mustard had been on the lake since before 7:00. He was at his most zealous, buzzing up and down the track in the tiny red Elfin racing car he used to test out the surface. He drove it with a sort of dedicated frenzy and, after one last look at the track, came roaring up toward Bluebird, the engine crackling in a cloud of pale blue smoke. Goggles glinting, crash helmet gleaming, salt in his red beard glistening, he leaned out of the cockpit to report the track clear and ready.

"It's all yours, Donald. It's flat and it's smooth."

Campbell nodded. "Fine. Fine, Andy," and turned to Ken Norris. "The recorder okay, Ken?"

"It's okay, Don."

"Are you sure you remembered the coffee, darling?" he said to Tonia as she handed him his helmet. "I missed my second cup at breakfast and I'll be ready for it when this is over."

He winked at her, but she said nothing and took his crepe-soled boots as he swung himself into the cockpit, then handed him the sneakers.

Because of the rush with which the new track had been laid, there had been no time to shift Bluebird's hangar and the rest of the base camp across from the southern end of the old main track. Instead it was left where it was, and a new road had been graded; it followed the old track for a couple of miles before turning right to meet the new track to the east.

Campbell took Bluebird up this road at a mere ninety. Several of us followed him in a cream-colored Morris 1100. Tonia was with us, sitting in the back with her embroidery, Campbell's boots, and Whacko the bear. She looked tense and nervous, which was unusual for her, and I saw that she had crumpled the corner of the linen she was embroidering and was still twisting it between her fingers.

The only time she spoke was when we were nearing the end of the service road and Bluebird, half a mile ahead of us, had begun to turn in a gentle arc to get onto the new track. It was exciting to see the car so close. It turned with a great sense of power and purpose. It seemed lithe and supple, and the movement was like that of a large animal before it springs.

"For God's sake, be careful," Tonia shouted suddenly. "D'you want to drive into him?" Again, it was unlike her to be so on edge, but we slowed right down and Wally Parr took a last photograph of Bluebird as Campbell accelerated and the blue car leaped away into the distance. Campbell was taking his greatest risk so far, and we sat in silence watching and wondering just how it would end.

Certainly Bluebird looked fast enough, although it is always difficult to judge speed at these levels, and there was still that ominous comet tail of yellow behind the car, which before had always meant that the track was disintegrating.

78

When Bluebird had disappeared over the horizon, we set off in pursuit, following her to the eastern end of the track.

"What was the speed?" Parr asked Norris.

"Around 250."

"That all?"

"Track again. He says there was trouble around the second-mile mark. We're going up in a minute to look." As an engineer, Norris has learned to treat disaster discreetly. He has an almost unnatural patience. The only sign of disappointment he would permit himself was to smile ruefully toward the car.

"So you won't have got the recorder readings you need from today's run?" said Parr.

"No." He drew the word out as if even a simple negative might be committing him to some unintentional inaccuracy. "Not yet, but let's wait and see what happens." He walked away, scratching his small mustache.

The inspection team was away nearly half an hour, and when they returned Villa and Norris looked particularly grim. Mustard had his sunglasses on again. Campbell did the talking.

"We seem to have torn up the surface even worse than I feared, and since this track is our lifeline we're not going to risk chopping it up now any more than we have to. So we intend to have one more run this morning and then we will leave the track for four or five days in the hope that the salt will harden and the ruts we've made will heal." ·

All this was said quite matter of factly, as if destroying the optimism and excitement with which the morning had begun was no concern of his. And Bluebird set off on the last run of the day.

This time it was fast, undeniably fast, and by the time Tonia reached him at the western end of the track he was out of the cockpit and shouted, "Two-ninety-five, darling." He smiled at her and she kissed him and said, "Well done, darling," and everyone was happy again.

And it *was* well done. He had almost achieved what he said he would. He had given the engineers the speed they required for their readings. And later that day news of this run of "practically 300 miles an hour" made the late editions of the evening papers in Adelaide. After all, as the news stories pointed out, it was the fastest a car had ever been driven in Australia.

So, in theory, Wednesday May 14th should have been celebrated as Campbell's best day since he arrived in Australia. Instead it was the start of the worst situation any record-breaker can find himself in.

For Campbell was no fool. Whatever his shortcomings, he knew about record-breaking, and at the end of that second run of his he understood as none of the rest of us could just how great the odds against him were.

All this showed in his face for a fraction of a second when the canopy lifted after the second run and he was in the cockpit and alone. He looked suddenly very old—not angry as I had seen him, or bitter as he had been after that last useless run on the main track, but old and very shaken. It was the way his mouth went, the way the lines suddenly accentuated themselves down the side of his face, the way he seemed to lose all expression, all his usual resilience. It was only a moment, but in that moment he seemed to understand that he was finally committed now to something his experience told him would almost certainly be fatal. With a successful run behind him, everyone, his supporters as well as those who disliked him and criticized him, would now expect him to continue on this death track.

Perhaps this was why he behaved as he did at the end of the run, brusquely shrugging aside the congratulations of the people who crowded around him. He stood talking to Leo

80

Villa for a while, serious-faced, sucking an empty Dunhill and watching as the little red compressor was started to drive the high-pressure water jet used for hosing away the salt from the car.

Then, more self-contained than ever, he was aboard his aircraft and circling away from the lake back to Muloorina.

No one else was in any hurry to get back to Muloorina. There were sandwiches in the hangar for anyone who wanted them and then, one by one, the cars and the Land Rovers began to trail off like late guests from a party that had gone on too long.

I drove back with Parr some time after 3:00. I think we exchanged no more than a dozen words during the whole journey, and as we approached Muloorina and saw the wind pump and the flat silver triangle of the homestead roof far out across the ochre-colored plain, a hot wind came up bringing flies and the pale gray dust into the cab of our truck.

Suddenly this dead, lost countryside seemed horribly appropriate for the drama we were involved in. It was all of a piece—the river that led nowhere, the hollow cry of the birds as we crossed the creek, the tin cans, bottles, sheep bones, packing cases half buried in the sand between the salt bushes and the outhouses. When the kangaroos were shot they were slung out here in the morning for the dogs to eat. And when trucks or pumps broke down for the last time, they were abandoned here, too, so that the land around the homestead was like a great dry cemetery littered with the remains of ancient trucks, cars, boilers, diesel engines. Bluebird may have cost more than all of them put together, but it would find a resting place here as comfortable as the rest.

"Well," said Parr, as he stopped the engine outside the homestead and lowered himself cautiously out of the cab, "something's got to happen, but I can't see what."

CHAPTER SEVEN

DURING that third week of May the winds began in earnest, great explosions of air as if the whole dry continent was suddenly on the move. The sky turned sick as the stifling clouds of umber-colored dust rumbled across the outback, and the same dust would come seeping beneath the flaps of tents and the mouths of sleeping bags and into hair and eyes and shaving soap and between the tufts of toothbrushes. There were another four days to wait while the lake dried out and Campbell's track was being prepared. And it was during these four days that things began to happen.

It started quite suddenly, this change of mood, although it had its origins in the layout of the camp—one of the many mistakes that were to dog Campbell during his time at Lake Eyre.

The camp was in two distinct parts. Campbell, his close friends, family, engineers, and retainers lived at the main homestead. Tonia and Leo's wife Joan were there to do the washing and the cooking, and there were chairs and tables and carpets on the floor and a bath with hot water that lasted with luck until around midday and a freezer for the beer. Life was crowded but tolerable enough.

But when the army arrived, under the arrangement Campbell had made with the Australian government, they decided

82

to pitch their tents on a ridge half a mile to the south, close to Elliot Price's landing strip. Certainly it was a good defensive position. There was a fine view from the ridge, and the army had set up six large green bell tents and a guard room and a first aid post and a generating unit and a canteen where green cans of Southwark bitter were sold in the evenings at two shillings a time.

At the moment the camp was still nothing like up to full strength. Just before the record attempt more troops would be sent from Adelaide to man the causeway, control the visitors, and carry out some of the heavy work involved. Until then the army camp was nearly empty and thus the obvious place to billet anyone for whom there was no room across at the homestead.

There were beds for them there, and army cooks ready to provide hot meals at any hour of the day or night. Army water trailers supplied first-rate field washing facilities, and at the correct regulation distance from the tents—far enough to keep away the flies but not too far to make the journey an ordeal—stood a neat row of twelve well-regulated army latrines, sweet and clean from the barrack stores in Adelaide. Up to a dozen men at a time could use them, sharing the view and the pleasure of each other's company.

With all these benefits the army camp naturally became the center for all the men who worked on the lake. Almost as a matter of course Andrew Mustard had parked his trailer nearby. So had one or two of his key personnel.

If the record had been won swiftly none of this would have mattered. But now with the dust storms and the wind and this latest delay, people suddenly noticed that Muloorina was split into two nations, one of which had cool beer and airplanes and lavatories that flushed, while the other had army cooking and canvas and twelve War Department thunder boxes. And during these few days toward the end of May,

83

the men in the army camp were getting tired of it. To them Campbell was increasingly a figure on the homestead verandah, a face at the window of the Aero Commander's cockpit.

When Bluebird actually ran, the camp drew together and discomforts were forgotten with the risks Campbell was taking. But he needed to be a hero now to be acceptable. As the delays piled up he turned into the Englishman every Australian secretly resents.

There was hardly any contact now between the two halves of the camp. Campbell never visited the canteen during the evening, but in his absence his every motive, every action was exhaustively discussed.

Parr had taken to going to the bar in the evenings to hear what was going on, and I would often see him there, a silent, slightly aloof figure on the edge of the crowd, drinking sweet Australian sherry and smiling to himself as he listened to the talk around him.

The inside of the tent was decorated with empty green beer cans threaded through strings and hung between the tent poles. There was a trestle table and a cash-box for whoever was serving, and a large oil drum for the evening's empties. The oil drum was already overflowing with empty cans when I arrived there.

"Why are we hanging around here now?" a fat young man in blue dungarees was shouting. The crowd round the table was considerable and it was hard to get a drink. When you got your beer you had to drink it from the can. There was a strong smell of creosote and male sweat, and the noise was overwhelming. But the man in the dungarees had a powerful voice.

"I'll tell you why. It's because Campbell's lost his nerve. Man, you can tell just by looking at him. He's petrified of the Goddamn car."

84

"Well, he drove it, didn't he?" said a voice. "Yesterday he drove it and he did 300."

"Too right he drove it," bellowed the blue dungarees. "Because he had to. Because everyone was pushing him. But 300 after we've been here nearly a month. What good is that, for God's sake? Why didn't he make a third run in that bloody great car of his and push on up to 350? The car'd do it. I tell you he's scared."

"And what about you?" said a young sergeant from the police. "I suppose you'd do it if you were in his place."

"That's not the point," he said. "What I'd do is not the point at all. I don't make the money he does. D'you know how much he's made out of this Bluebird? Bloody millions, just as his old man did before him. I tell you he's boxing clever with his backers. He's not in this business for fun. He's in for money, and he'll just spin it out again as he did last year."

"But be fair," said the sergeant. "Either he's scared or he's boxing clever, but he can't be both."

"Why not?" shouted the other man, getting red in the face, "I don't see why not. I wouldn't put anything past him."

"No, you've got it wrong. It's not like that at all." The voice was quiet, restrained, and its very softness made an impressive answer to the other man's bluster. The speaker was a fair-haired, rather solid man who worked for Andrew Mustard on the lake.

"I don't see how you can say he's scared. He got the water record six times and you don't get a scared man doing that. But I think he's sick. I think that Utah crash did more damage than we've heard about. And I think it's left him with a psychological block about really fast speeds. The closer he gets to the speed he crashed at Utah, the more of a nightmare it will be for him."

Parr finished his beer and got up. As I walked back toward his quarters with him, he was at his most enigmatic.

"The English are supposed to take their pleasures sadly," he said. "As an Australian I try to take other people's sadnesses pleasurably. Come and have a drink. I've something to show you."

As usual he was wearing a hat with a mosquito net. Along with his army boots and surplus denim trousers, this gave him a serious dedicated air. His room, for which the Australian Associated Press was paying Elliot Price only slightly less than if their employee had been staying at Claridge's, was in a long, corrugated iron hut, and was conveniently close to the mobile post office through which he filed his copy to Sydney. It had a cement floor, a chair, and a large iron bedstead with a prolapsed mattress. And with that obscure ability to make himself comfortable anywhere, which is perhaps the surest mark of nature's newspapermen, he had filled it with his personal collection of paperbacks, old socks, shaving equipment, bottles, transistor radios, and spare pairs of trousers. His typewriter was on the chair and he had just started reading Mary McCarthy's book *The Group*.

"D'you know," he said, as he poured three quarters of an inch of Johnny Walker for me into his Pepsodent-tasting mug, "this ridiculous book is actually banned in the worthy state of Victoria, and as a result there's not a housewife in Melbourne who hasn't read it. Australia must be one of the last places in the world where the authorities really give one an incentive to read serious literature."

"It looks as though you'll have time to get through it, anyhow," I said.

"I'm not so sure there won't be other things to do. I've a hunch things are just starting to get interesting now. You see, he's in a trap, isn't he—and one he's made for himself. He should have been satisfied with his boat and his water records. But he wasn't. Heroes never are. They have to go on proving something to themselves. Fame is as habit-forming as heroin

86

and twice as deadly. I suppose that's why he overreached himself and took on this great car—pride, conceit, the classic formula for self-destruction in all the best tragedies.

"Take this business of the crash at Utah, for instance. I should have thought of it a long time ago, but this afternoon I paid a call on Ken Norris and asked him about it. He lent me this."

He rummaged among the litter of papers and magazines on the end of the bed and produced a thin, gray-covered folder. Typed on the front was the title: "Campbell–Norris 7. Land Speed Record Attempt 1960. Report No. 60/18D/R.1."

"I was looking through it before dinner," he said. "Take a look for yourself, and excuse me if I remove my boots while you're reading. I think page eight is the part that will interest you."

The report had been run off on a duplicator and the type-written pages had blurred slightly, although they were perfectly legible. I began to read from it:

Bonneville Salt Flats—Friday, September 16, 1960. *Run 5. South to North. Start approx. 6.22* A.M.

Wind was gusting 3 to 6 mph. from SSE as the car was wound up to 9,500 compressor revolutions per minute and D.M.C. pulled away well to the right hand of the central black line to miss the pothole at mile 1. Ambient temperature was down to 17°C, so relatively good engine performance was expected.

D.M.C.'s comments at the end of the run were as follows:

(a) Speed at the end of three miles—300 mph. (K. W. Norris reminded D.M.C. that 300 mph was required in 2 miles for the record.)

(b) C.r.p.m. up to 10,000 plus.

(c) Stopping procedure. Engine cut—air brakes out, foot brakes on 120-lb./sq. in. at 7½ mile mark—speed down from 260 to 95 mph in 3 miles. Mechanical brakes very good indeed.

(d) Jet pipe temperature reached 600°C max.

(e) Steering was light and the car wanted to wander off.

In general everyone was very happy with the run.... D.M.C. again requested that during Run 6 he should try both the acceleration of the car and also braking hard at the other end.

"It's run number six that's the important one," said Parr. "Very strange style these engineers use when they're writing their reports. D.M.C. is short for Campbell."

About 1.6 miles [*i.e.* 1.5 miles from mile 0, there being 0.1 miles from mile 0 to the start of the run] up the course, C.N.7 [the official abbreviation for the car] started to go off track, finishing nearly broadside on at 1.9 miles in a spiral left-hand slide. From then on the car took off for nearly 200 yards, bouncing several times before coming to rest approximately 500 yards away on the salt to the left of the course and into the wind.

But Ken Norris had obviously thought that the occasion demanded something more than this, and had added the following first person account:

7.10 A.M. and as C.N.7 pulled away it was obvious that she was accelerating very fast and Leo and I made a quick dash for our Rover follow-up car, which was parked about 20 yards away facing the course. We were quickly up to 90 mph on the right-hand side of the right-hand marker line but C.N.7 was by then a speck on the horizon. Suddenly there appeared to be more "dust" than usual surrounding C.N.7 and then from this cloud a blue object flew upward. My immediate thought was that the top plenum chamber cover had flown off and I cursed inwardly for not doing more stringent tests. My immediate reaction, that the Skipper would be okay if it was indeed the top cover, was quickly dispelled as the cloud had now increased considerably and appeared to be way to the left-hand of the course. Leo's comment was "My God, he's in trouble," and I prayed "Please God he's all right," as Leo plunged across the track heading straight for the cloud.

We were doing a good 90 mph and it took us a mere 60 seconds to reach what was left of the car, but those 60 seconds seemed endless. The past kept imposing itself with endless accusations. You should have done this and that and that!!! I don't remember anything of the wreckage on the way across the salt, my eyes being fixed on the black blob ahead. As we drew near, it seemed that C.N.7 was upside down and I felt sick and empty inside—but closer still and it was apparent that she was the right way up, and as Leo was screeching to a halt I was preparing to jump from the doorway. I could think of nothing but reaching the canopy and yanking it up. I could see Donald's head nodding to and fro dazedly inside, the crash helmet looked weird and ungainly. Another leap and I yanked the canopy external release at the front end. A jump and I was on the wreck at the back end of the canopy and trying to pry up the perspex. Leo was now at the front and he pulled the release again and the canopy came up easily.

Blood was spattered on places over the Skipper's blue overalls, but he seemed okay otherwise. Consciousness of the engine running sweetly impelled me to action again and I skipped down the far side of the canopy and grabbed across the cockpit for the emergency fuel cut-off. Nothing happened and Leo and I pulled on the release together. The engine stopped and Peter Carr was leaning over the far side of the cockpit to release the harness. Tonia was running across the salt, her legs dragging slower and slower as she approached. Thumbs up and a short "he's okay" and she came on again as strong arms were dragging the Skipper free. The ambulance was now alongside, the stretcher was out and Tonia was hovering over the Skipper as he mumbled, "I seem to have clouted my ear" on the way to the ambulance.

"Go away, pressmen, can't you see he's hurt? No, we don't know what's happened yet."

The ambulance pulled away and we gazed dumbfounded at what a few seconds past was to be the fastest car in the world.

Dejection followed as we wandered slowly back through scattered wreckage to the course and the start of the trouble.

I looked across at Parr. Miss McCarthy seemed to be claiming all his attention.

"Finished?" he asked, without taking his eyes from the

book. "Hardly what you'd expect from our friend Norris, is it?"

The hall was tiny and packed with an obscure smell of dust and good works, and Tonia sang for over an hour. There was no stage in the mission hall at Marree but that hardly worried her, and she sang before her audience of storekeepers and sheepmen's wives as if her life depended on it. She was a great success. The applause was enthusiastic.

She had agreed to give this performance to raise funds for the mission in the local aborigine settlement, and when she sang it was uncanny the way she suddenly turned into a person none of us had seen at Lake Eyre. The illusion was total. She could have been in Paris or Las Vegas, and she sang as if she was proving to herself that there was a world outside the nightmare of Lake Eyre. She could still make an audience respond as she had done so many times before, still be the controlled professional self that all her training had made her.

Marree is the nearest thing to "High Noon" to be found these days outside the Middle West, and as we came from the hall we passed the aborigine cattlemen strolling through the late afternoon dust in their high-heeled boots on the way from the stockyard, and saw the small, neat clapboard houses and the tethering posts for the horses along the main street. And before driving back to Muloorina we had a drink at the Bar Marree ("Konstantinos Sideris, Licensed Dealer in Wines and Spirits"). It was a long, bleak, unlovely room with shining apple-green walls and a linoleum-covered bar and fluorescent lighting on the ceiling and a large black notice beside the advertisements for Craven Filter saying, "If you have not reached the age of twenty-one please do not order liquor as the penalty is severe."

Tonia was happy and relaxed after her performance, and the strain that had begun to show during the last few days at

Muloorina had vanished entirely. She was smiling now and her face was very sunburned.

"I had almost forgotten how much I need to work," she said. "It's bad for me if I don't sing. My career is really as important to me as Donald's is to him, and when all this is over I'll be picking it up again. I've a recording contract in Paris and then a lot of work in New York. You know," she said, "Donald used to be very jealous of my work and when I married him I gave it all up. There was a part in a musical on Broadway and a film with David Niven, too. They both went. It was a great mistake. You see, no woman can stand the strain of all this unless she has another life as well. His first two wives couldn't take it. One of the reasons I can is that I've got my career back again now, and when all this is over I'll just go off on tour and sing."

Lake Eyre could have been a whole continent away.

"The secret of staying married to Donald," she went on, "is not to be demanding. The more demanding a woman becomes the more elusive he is, and if I ever became an ordinary housewife he'd get bored and that would be that."

"That's hardly likely," I said.

She nodded but did not smile. "No, you're right there."

She was silent then and stood sipping her lemonade and watching the beginning of a fight at the far end of the bar among some men from the railway.

"Now, boys. Now, boys," shouted the barman. "Just cut it out, boys. I'm not losing me license because of you. Now cut it out." He was a small hairless man with an impressive voice, and order was restored.

"We're different from other people," she said at last. "That's the truth of it. Donald's not like any ordinary husband and I'm not like any ordinary wife. We're restless, crazy, obsessed sort of people. At times it's hell and at times it's wonderful.

"Look at Donald now. D'you think I enjoy being with him and watching him at a time like this? D'you think I don't want to tell him twenty times a day to get out of Lake Eyre and forget it and settle down somewhere and start enjoying life again? But winning this record is part of him. He's got to do it and no one will stop him.

"Perhaps you think I don't know the danger he's in. Believe me, I know it. I live every minute of it when he's in that car. But it's something he has to go through and I have to go through it with him. You know Donald," she said. "Can you imagine what he'd be like for the rest of his life if he left Lake Eyre now?"

"I saw an old newsreel," she went on. "A very old one of Donald as a small boy greeting his father on his return from Daytona with a new record. It was the time Sir Malcolm got his knighthood, I think. And this picture of Donald was one of the saddest things I've ever seen. There he was, this very English schoolboy on the quay at Southampton—his hair brushed, his best suit on, excited out of his life. Then there was a shot of Sir Malcolm coming down the gangplank— smiling, successful, surrounded by admirers and reporters—a real hero, and my poor Donald never got a look in. You could see him on the edge of the crowd trying to catch his father's attention, desperately trying to reach him, but never quite managing it.

"I think Donald is still that small boy," she said. "And now his ambition ruins most of the things that make a normal man happy. If he gave up now he would never forgive himself— or me."

Work on the lake continued for the rest of that week. The rumors continued, and we all waited.

On Sunday, May 24th, for the first time since we had been at Muloorina, the lake was visible at dawn from the homestead like a thin silver thread along the horizon.

"Bad sign," Elliot Price said at breakfast, "for you, Don,

not for me. Funny when you think of it. A good shower of rain now would finish everything for you here, but it could be worth ten or twenty thousand pounds to me in extra food for the sheep."

"For crying out loud," said Campbell. "You mean there's always rain when you can see the lake?"

"Not always, Don. Not always. Can't rely on anything in this part of the world—not even rain. Rest yourself, Don. It'll probably not come to anything. Any rain you get up here is a miracle."

"Well, I've been getting rather too many of your miracles lately, thank you very much." He had a pinched look and his blue sweater had a cigarette burn on the shoulder and had come unstitched under the left armpit.

I strolled onto the verandah with him, and a small girl in a white straw hat suddenly appeared from nowhere and asked him for his autograph. She was a round-faced child with freckles and large silent eyes. Her family were friends of the Prices and had driven over from Marree in the hope of seeing Bluebird.

"Why do you want my autograph?" asked Campbell, suddenly squatting down beside the child. "Do you collect autographs?"

The child nodded.

"Why do you collect autographs?"

She would not answer him for a while, but Campbell waited patiently.

"I'm starting my collection with yours," she explained solemnly, "and when I get home I will stick it in a book so you'll be the very first."

"What's your name then?" asked Campbell.

"Lindy."

And carefully, elaborately, on a sheet of paper from one of his notebooks he wrote, "Lindy, lots of love, Donald Campbell." He wrote it in radiant blue ink and the capital D and the capital C were large and flowing. "Donald doesn't write his signature, he paints it," one of his friends once said. The little girl seemed very happy.

"I used to sell the old man's autographs at school," he said when the child had gone. "He found out in the end. He found out most things. Asked how much I was getting. I told him two shillings. 'Heavens, boy,' he said, 'that's not enough. Should be ten shillings at least!'"

He paused and looked serious again. "I hear they've started talking about Utah," he said. "I thought they would."

He lowered himself carefully into an old blue and white deckchair and began filling his pipe from a pigskin tobacco pouch.

"Have they got round to saying yet that I've lost my nerve?"

"Yes."

"There's always someone says that if you get held up on a record bid longer than a week or two. In 1955 we were held up nearly six months at Ulswater trying to persuade the hydroplane to go through the water barrier. You should have heard what one or two charitable people called me then."

He settled himself comfortably, got his feet onto a box of canned peas, then turned his attention to persuading his pipe to light. "But this talk about Utah is something new. What are they saying?"

"A lot of loose talk. You don't have to take any notice of it."

"No, I want to know." The pale eyes were watching me closely now through the clouds of fresh smoke.

I told him. "They're saying that the Utah crash has left you with a sort of phobia about really high speeds and that you'll never risk approaching the same speed again."

"Ah," he said, nodding. "So that's it."

He was silent for a while still sucking away at his pipe. Then he shifted and looked at me again.

94

"D'you want to know what really happened?" he said.

"Only if you want to tell me."

"It was a strange business—a very strange business, believe you me. You see, when I took Bluebird out to Bonneville in 1960 I went convinced that I was going to kill myself. I had a presentiment of death when I was on vacation in Majorca just before I started the trip. It's the one time in my life I've had it, and sure enough everything went wrong from then on.

"I remember it all so well. At the start of that second run I had felt almost light-headed with excitement, totally without fear. I gave Bluebird all she'd got and saw the speedometer reading 320—320, mark you—as the *first*-mile marker flashed past.

"Damn good, I said to myself, old Ken will be pleased. But then, *then*, instead of slackening off and going back very pleased with myself as I had every right to be, I put my foot down harder still. Madness."

He thumped his knee and paused a moment, glaring into space. "Sheer madness.

"I knew she was going out of control. Felt it. Actually felt the tail slipping. And I knew what would happen. I knew we'd crash but none of it seemed to concern me. I just sat there in that split second thinking, 'well, this is the end,' and not feeling the remotest interest.

"The rest you know. The car took off, shot nearly a thousand yards, miraculously staying the right way up, and bumped six times on the deck before coming to a standstill. When Ken and old Leo opened up the canopy I was unconscious, of course, covered in blood. I'd had one hell of a crack on the head, but I was alive and I came to in the ambulance.

"The first thing I remember after the crash was seeing Tonia, bless her heart, peering through the window at me from the front of the ambulance, and hearing old Peter Carr, my project manager saying, 'Wave to her, Don. She's worried stiff. Wave to her and show her you're all right.'

"So I waved and did my best to smile and said, 'Tell her the old family jewels are still intact.' And at the hospital, when they tried carting me in on a stretcher, I said, 'Not on your sweet life. The Bluebird project's not ending with a picture in all the evening papers of yours truly on a stretcher.' So I held on to old Peter and just managed to make it through that hospital door on my own pins.

"But why had it happened? What had made me behave like that?"

He stopped and looked at me as if I ought to know the answer for myself. "Oxygen," he said finally. "The oxygen I'd been breathing at the time of the crash. On the advice of several experts we had fitted an oxygen breathing system to the car and, as we discovered much later, there are certain people—and of course I had to be one of them—who experience a form of drunkenness if they inhale pure oxygen at sea level.

"It was as simple as that. I had been inhaling pure oxygen throughout the two runs and all the symptoms fitted in with those we found in reports of experiments on combat pilots during the war—elation, loss of all sense of fear and reality, slowing down of reaction—the whole works. They call it oxygen poisoning."

"But what about the effect the crash had on you—the nervous trouble. How bad was that?"

"John, it was something I wouldn't wish on my worst enemy. It was terrifying. If I hadn't lived through it, I would never have believed it was possible."

He paused, discovered his pipe was out, and leaned forward to relight it.

"When they got me inside that hospital they seemed to

96

think at first there was nothing much the matter with me apart from cuts and severe shock and concussion. They X-rayed me, but the real damage to the skull didn't show up. It was only when cerebral spinal fluid started trickling out of my ear that one of the doctors said, 'Hey, this man has fractured the base of his skull. He's lucky to be alive at all.'

"It took a long time to get over. A very long time, believe you me. For several months after the crash I was like an old man, terrified of anything out of the ordinary. I couldn't so much as drive a car. I didn't want to meet people. It was agony for me to make any decision. All I could do was to stay at home, and the only real relief was in bed.

"Then it began to lift. I didn't look quite so ghastly and I was able to get on a little with the business of rebuilding Bluebird and starting up the whole project again."

"But you never had any doubts about wanting another try at the record?" I asked.

He seemed surprised. "Doubts? No, why? The only thing to do was to go on. But I can tell you it was no easy matter getting a new car built. The old one was a complete write-off. During 1961 and 1962 there were some fairly frantic periods of overwork, and that was when I found the nervous attacks recurring. They'd take the form of unimaginable fear. Totally and utterly without reason. I'd just be certain suddenly that I was going to die."

"And when did you have the last attack?"

"Oh, a long time ago. This brain business tends to right itself with time if you're lucky. I've been lucky."

May's last week began, and the trouble that had been getting closer and closer to the deceptively quiet surface of life at Muloorina came bubbling up. It began on Monday evening. The telephone in the sitting room started ringing, and there was a journalist from Sydney on the line asking for Campbell.

"There's a report in a London paper that because of the delays and the trouble you've run into, your most important backers are pulling out, Mr. Campbell. Have you any comment you would like to make at this stage?"

"Totally and completely untrue," replied Campbell. "I said, sir, that the report is totally and completely untrue. Your source of information is seriously misinformed." There was a pause. "I said it's rubbish, sir. I have no backers so I fail to see how they could have pulled out. If they are referring to the association I had with the British Petroleum Company, that ended by mutual consent nearly six months ago. I am financing this attempt out of my own pocket. Good night to you, sir."

He replaced the telephone carefully and stayed sitting in the armchair for some while without speaking to anyone.

This meant real trouble now. Denials were no use with a story like this, although everything he had said on the telephone was true. He had no backers in the normal sense of the term, no sympathetic financiers or industrialists supplying him with money that could be suddenly cut off as the Sydney reporter had suggested. His long association with British Petroleum (under which the oil company had pumped its estimated quarter of a million pounds into the Bluebird project in return for the right to exploit Campbell and any records he won for advertising purposes) had ended in December 1963 when Campbell rejected the company's proposal to put their own manager in charge of the Bluebird project and pay Campbell all his expenses plus a handsome bonus on attaining the record.

"You can only have one man in charge of an operation like this," Campbell had said at the time. "I've never heard of a record yet that was won by a committee."

His subsequent agreement with Ampol was a straight-forward deal under which the Australian oil company supplied him with his fuel and oil and paid a lump sum for the right to advertise the fact that they were doing so. The same sum again was promised if he got the record. And all the rest of the money he had been promised from outside sources depended now on the record. And if he failed?

"If I fail this time, old scout," he had said in a moment of sudden candor, "I shall be a very poor man."

He must have been thinking of this later that night when he called an unexpected meeting up at the army camp "just to put the record straight." Mysteriously the news about backers pulling out had already got around the entire camp. Nobody quite knew what it meant but the phrase sounded convincing and by now many people were ready to believe that the attempt was about to fold.

There was a touch of desperation about the way he spoke. He was wearing a new dark blue quilted nylon parka he had ordered from a store in Adelaide.

"I would like to tell you all that some misinformed individuals have been spreading totally false information about the Bluebird project and saying that certain 'backers' are withdrawing their support. I don't know, gentlemen, where this information has come from, but I would like to state here and now that it is totally and completely incorrect."

He paused to look at the ring of faces surrounding him. Mustard was in the front row. Parr was to the left, and Superintendent Brebner was standing by the entrance to the tent, his gaunt sad face overtopping the crowd in front. But there was no reaction from anyone, and Campbell continued in silence.

"Whatever difficulties we have had to encounter, gentlemen, I still intend to go forward toward the record slowly, determinedly, scientifically."

99

He shifted now and stood facing us sternly. "No record, gentlemen, has ever been won without a struggle."

But struggles alone were not enough that week. Despite all Campbell's denials, several Sydney papers appeared next morning with two-inch front-page headlines announcing that his backers *were* pulling out. And when he tried a run with Bluebird on Tuesday morning on the track Mustard's men had now widened, he complained that it was "like driving over old bricks," and his top speed was 250 miles an hour.

Campbell slept most of that afternoon, and appeared in the sitting room in search of a drink around 5:30. He looked rested and assured.

"I've been thinking about the old man," he said, "and wondering what he would have done in my place. He probably wouldn't have put up with this present caper for one moment. He wouldn't have stayed being knocked about by Lake Eyre. He'd have been out of here like a dose of salts. But you see, I've got to stay now. Things are rather different for me."

He leaned against the mantelpiece by one of the vases of plastic lilacs and carefully poured himself a vodka and tonic, half an inch of vodka, the rest tonic.

"He was without question the greatest man I've ever known. He was the best at this game and no one's ever equaled him. He could be very formidable when he wanted to, my father. Very, very formidable."

He sipped his drink, then held the glass up to inspect it.

"I don't drink much these days, you know. The old tum's not really up to wine or beer any more. Old age, I suppose. Catches up with you in many ways. The reactions begin to slow down a bit although you make up for that in experience if you're sensible. That's what Father did—used his sense and his experience and cut down the element of chance. He was built to last. You know he was fifty-four in 1939 when he got his last record, and if it hadn't been for the war he'd have carried on longer still.

"I've asked Andrew Mustard and all his boys in for a drink before dinner," he said casually. "If we're going to get the record now, that track's got to be smoother and they're the only people who can do it."

Just then Andrew Mustard arrived. He looked shy and unwell.

"Good evening, Mr. Mustard," said Campbell, "and good evening, gentlemen," he said as the rest of Mustard's team filed into the room. It was the first time they had been to the homestead for a drink like this and some of them had put on ties for the occasion.

When everyone was seated the Johnnie Walker was passed silently around. There was the muffled crack and hiss of beer cans opening, and people shifted uneasily in their seats wondering exactly what Campbell was up to now. He looked carefully at all those faces before he spoke.

"Gentlemen, we're up against it." He was earnest, a little unsure of himself. "The car can do it. I believe *I* can do it. But on top of that we need a miracle and it is a miracle that only you gentlemen can perform. I have got to gamble on your ability to get the salt of the new track as smooth for its whole length as it is for the first three miles.

"Now I know this is asking the impossible of you, but believe me, we need the impossible. And if it makes you feel any happier, I'm prepared to put five hundred pounds in the kitty to be shared among you."

He paused and lit his pipe. If he was expecting any reaction to his offer, none came. No one in the room moved. I watched Andrew Mustard. He was sitting on the sofa, and

101

the line of china geese on the wall behind him looked as if they were flying out of his head. The lilacs on the mantelpiece seemed to have grown.

Campbell stood and waited for a reply and the silence lengthened. It was one of those crucial moments when people's opinions are in the balance and almost anything can be said.

Someone cleared his throat. More eyes were turned toward Andrew Mustard and for a moment it seemed as if he was going to speak. Instead, by yet another minor freak of circumstance, the large mahogany clock that was the pride of the Prices' mantelpiece chose this point to strike 7:00 and the moment was lost.

Instead of the criticism and the distrust coming out then and being dealt with, point by point, as it still might have been, it stayed where it was. Stan Dibben said something about the need for the greatest urgency in going for the record once the work on the track was finished. Campbell said of course no one was more aware of the need for urgency than he was.

That was that, and Campbell seemed to think he had won. As the Johnnie Walker began its second journey, he began speaking again and his voice was steadier, more confident than before. He insisted now on the need for fifteen clear runs in Bluebird so that the engineers would have a chance to test and adjust the car all the way up to the record.

"Give me those runs, gentlemen, on a track like a billiard table and I will promise you the record. Some people have been saying I should put my foot down right now and get the record that way. But believe me, that's not the way. That's the way to smash the car and probably the pilot, too. I tried it once at Utah four years ago when I was drunk on oxygen. I'm not doing it again."

It was an impressive speech.

"One last thing, gentlemen. It is now Tuesday. This weekend I'm getting the time-keepers up. I will not run on that track until you tell me it's ready. But as soon as you do, you will have the satisfaction of knowing that every run I make over 300 will be timed officially. And I would like to remind you that in this game we don't make records. We make timed trials over measured distances."

That night the dogs that slept outside the homestead were kept awake until after midnight by the noise of hammering and a weird blue light sputtering from one of the outbuildings. Tom Scrimshire was welding a pair of new drags for smoothing the track, and before dawn they were on their way to the lake.

The rain that was forecast passed to the east and then down to Port Augusta and Adelaide, and by Friday night Mustard reported that the track was nearly ready. It was hard and smooth for something over eleven miles. The worst point lay where it crossed the old track at the south end but there was hope that even this could be improved.

It was on Friday, too, that the first of the time-keepers arrived. They spent Saturday on the lake with the official surveyor, measuring Campbell's mile to the nearest half inch, and setting up tripods for the cameras, which were synchronized with an electronic clock to measure the car's entrance and exit through the mile to a thousandth of a second.

Official stewards were still needed before Campbell could set a new record, but they were due to arrive any time now. On Saturday evening Campbell announced that he would be making his first timed run early the following morning.

"Perhaps I was wrong," said Parr that night. "Perhaps he's really got a chance after all."

CHAPTER EIGHT

ON the last Sunday in May Campbell rose just after 6:00, breakfasted on toast and coffee, and decided to drive the Morris 1100 to the lake himself. He was calm. He was silent. And as he drove the Morris with such assurance through the dust, the morning haze, across the flat, dry countryside to Lake Eyre, he looked ready at last to do what he had to do. The sun had risen. The salt glittered gold and pink and his task seemed suddenly very simple. He would drive the car, he would get what he wanted, and none of the criticisms, none of the doubts, none of the memories of childhood and fears of middle age would matter any longer.

We rumbled along the battered road to the causeway, slowed down to pass through the checkpoint the army was manning to keep unauthorized visitors from the lake.

"Good luck," shouted the military police sergeant as he waved us through. "Good luck," shouted the corporal in the large wideawake hat.

"Why do they have to say that," Campbell muttered under his breath. "It's always unlucky." And he went on to tell how the old waterman at Lake Coniston had said "good luck" to him just before he drove his boat in 1951 and hit the submerged log at 180. "He'd never said good luck to me before, and afterward I asked him why he did then. He said he never knew."

104

At the base camp there was a new atmosphere. Bluebird was already out of the hangar and ready to run, and everyone seemed to have a measure of goodwill for Campbell.

Mustard had been buzzing up and down the track in his red torpedo of a racing car to test the surface. The time-keepers' photoelectric apparatus was between the seventh-and eighth-mile mark.

"Everything's ready, Donald," said Mustard, wiping the salt from his beard and smiling his faint smile. "You'll never get the track any better than it is today. She's hard and she's smooth."

Campbell nodded and said nothing.

"Okay, Skipper?" asked Villa, bustling forward. "Everything okay? It looks a good day for a run."

And it did. It seemed as if after all the false starts Lake Eyre was going to play straight with Campbell at last and allow him to try for his record on even terms.

Everything went smoothly, and Campbell was in the cockpit, just completing his check-through, when a fault was discovered in one of the brake calipers for the front wheel. It was not serious. Normally it would have taken half an hour to change, but through an oversight the only spare was back at Muloorina, and it was 11:00 before the spare had been collected, fitted, tested, and the car was ready to run again.

It was the wrong time to have a delay. Campbell had two and a half hours to worry about the military policeman who had wished him luck and the boatman who had done the same thirteen years earlier at Coniston. Mustard had two and a half hours to worry about the surface of the new track. "In this heat, Donald, I suggest we should specifically ban any runs after midday. Already you will find it considerably softer than it was at eight."

Worst of all, the mood changed. We drank coffee. We waited. Campbell signed a few autographs for visitors and chatted to Tonia and watched the engineers as they worked away, stripping down the front wheel assembly. By the time he was back in the cockpit and ready to move off again, the promise had gone from the day.

For the first run Campbell chose the north end. This gave several of us a chance to wait by the measured mile to see him pass. We had the Morris 1100 again. Wally Parr was with us, wearing very large sunglasses with gold rims. The combination of these with the mosquito net on his hat was disturbing. Tonia was with us too, huddled into the back seat, looking tense and white-faced as she tried to hold Campbell's boots and Whacko the teddy bear and keep her fingers crossed all at the same time. She was wearing a red, white, and blue striped shirt and blue silk slacks. Her hair was tied with white ribbon, and she looked pretty and out of her element, as if she had finally given up trying to understand why her husband had to be here.

The control radio the Morris carried began its pedantic squawking from the front seat, as the track controller at the north end of the course told the time-keepers to get ready.

"Mobile One to time-keepers. The torch is alight. Bluebird is rolling." And we waited, straining our eyes to that strange horizon where the mirages danced above the salt islands, and the only landmarks were the spider's-web lattice of the film towers and the yellow cubes of the mile markers along the track. We waited for that small black dot to appear, a dot that would come skimming toward us out of nothingness and only at the last moment metamorphose itself into the blue snout, fish tail, haunched wheel fairings of the car, before speeding away down the measured mile, past the tripod legs of the time-keepers' apparatus, trailing its thin yellow tail of salt.

No one in the car said anything, and before Campbell was

106

past we had started the engine and raced away to be there as soon as he opened the cockpit.

When we got to Bluebird she was resting alone. It was the first time I had seen the car stationary on the salt without something near it, and it looked unearthly in the middle of such emptiness—the only object, the only sign of life—and as the cockpit lid rose it was like watching the first movement from a rocket that had landed on a new planet.

But when we ran over, and peered in at him as he sat there with his silver crash helmet still on, he wore an expression I had seen several times before.

"Well, we are in dire trouble," he said, without looking at any of us. He lifted off his helmet, handed it to Tonia still without speaking directly to anyone. His voice had a resigned impersonal note to it, as if he were reporting something that had nothing particularly to do with him.

"At 320, just before the measured mile, I got high frequency vibrations so badly that I could hardly see, let alone steer properly. It was as much as I could do to hang onto the wheel, and the whole car was bumping so hard that the track was a blur."

Disaster seemed to call out a particular eloquence in him, and the cameras around him began to click, making immortal his despair on squares of colored celluloid. From the Morris came the sound of the radio as it clacked the queries of the check points across the lonely ether. "Mobile Two to Project One. What are further intentions? Please inform additional movements. Over."

Campbell had heaved himself onto the back of the cockpit and lit a cigarette. He smoked grimly, as if drawing a bitter wisdom from the tobacco. He continued his impersonal narrative of disaster.

"There was some discrepancy between the air speed indicator and the speedometer on the dashboard, but I estimate

Bluebird was doing something just over 310 when the vibrations started. The vibrations themselves were at around 300 cycles a second. I cut power at once and eased her down. There was nothing else to be done. The frequency was so great that at first I thought something must be broken. It was like nothing I've experienced before except in the boat at very high speed."

He finished his cigarette and no one spoke. I saw Andrew Mustard looking at him intently, but he said nothing.

"It felt as if the wheels could be out of balance, Ken," Campbell said.

But Andrew Mustard assured Norris that all the wheels had been accurately balanced before the run. Campbell repeated the question, but Mustard shook his head.

Other possibilities for the vibrations were gloomily considered. Norris scratched his chin with his pencil and began calculations on his pad to see if they could be explained by the twisting of the half shaft and there was talk of possible trouble with the suspension. Finally it was decided to reduce tire pressures from 145 to 125 pounds per square inch. At least it was action of a sort.

The big army wrecker truck drew up, and the REME men manning it looked like troops after a surrender. One of them, but only one, lit a cigarette. The skull and horns of a large buffalo had been attached to the radiator, and in that bright sunlight the skull seemed to grin at the long useless shape of the blue car.

"How fast did you say, Donald?" asked Evan Green, the project manager, a good-looking conciliatory man who held the record for driving all around Australia. "Three twenty?"

"Well, old chum, there was this ten mile an hour discrepancy between the two instruments."

I walked away from the car. It was 1:20 in the afternoon. The sun was very hot, the salt bright gold. The cars in the distance seemed to drown in the mirage as if in water. Men turned into black insects clambering across the glare.

Wally Parr joined me and we strolled over to one of the trucks where he had left a thermos of tea.

Pat Crowe was there, the solid young photographer from the *Adelaide Advertiser,* who looks like the last King of Romania on the stamps they issued before he was deposed.

"What Campbell needs," said Parr, "is not another car or another track, but a good psychoanalyst." We nodded. It was probably unjust, but it relieved our feelings.

"But if he really did feel the vibrations," said Crowe slowly, "I can't say I blame him. If it happened to me at 300 miles an hour, I know damn well I'd chop the power."

Parr's thermos had a fawn lid, which unscrewed to form two cups. He filled one and handed it to me.

"But that's just the point," said Parr. "You and I are not doing it. We've not been paid to do it. He has. It's his responsibility. All these years he has been getting his name in the papers. Now he's got to deliver. And you know why he's been getting his name in the papers. Just because he's supposed *not* to be like the rest of us. A real record-breaker can't allow himself the reactions of an ordinary man. This was his chance to prove all his critics wrong, and he's bungled it."

He poured himself some tea. It was the first time I had seen him angry. He took off his hat and his sunglasses and glared at Bluebird in the distance.

"But what you're asking is that the man should be willing to kill himself," said Pat Crowe. "That's too much. You can't ask any man to do that."

"That's his job. That's always been the job of these record-breakers. They all had to be willing to kill themselves, otherwise there wouldn't have been any records. D'you think Cobb would have chopped power just now? D'you think his father would?"

Bluebird was still sitting where she had rested—elegant, ludicrous, unloved. Small men in white overalls bustled round her.

"I'm sure that every time they set a record, they did so by going just that bit beyond what they thought a man could survive. That's why they were famous, and that's why there were records. And that's what this man won't do. And that's why he's not a record-breaker and why we might as well all go home."

He finished his tea, threw away the dregs from the cup on the salt, and carefully replaced his hat.

"So you want it to be a blood sport," I said.

"Of course I do. Record-breaking must be a blood sport, otherwise it's not record-breaking and there's no point to it. If there's no risk to the damned driver anyone could get a record simply by paying a million or so for a new car, and if that's all it is, you might as well spend your million on sound-test equipment and set up your record in the laboratory. You'll learn a lot more that way."

The technicians had finished by now. The sandwiches of cheese, corned beef, and lettuce had been bolted down, and Campbell announced that, late as it was, he would try one more run to test out the release mechanism for the safety parachute.

We went back to the Morris 1100, and waited once again to see if the run would be any different this time. But it was slower, and when we reached Bluebird at the end of the track we found that he had applied brakes, air brakes, and parachute.

This time nobody asked questions and nobody bothered to take pictures. Tom Scrimshire had a toothache, and began gloomily winding up the parachute from where it had trailed behind the car.

110

Later than usual, Leo Villa came puffing up, looking solider, more loyal than ever.

"Everything okay, Skipper, that time?" he called out.

"Pretty rough, Unc. Pretty rough."

"That's the lot of them for today, Skipper?"

"That's the lot now, Unc. I'll drive her down the course under her own power and then back to base."

As we followed him back to the base camp, the whole nature of what we were all up to suddenly became clear. It was not a record bid we were watching. It was not just a car trying to go faster than any car had ever gone before. We were watching the trial of a man. The car, the wind, the surface of the lake, were merely instruments on which to test him like the hazards of medieval justice when a man was put to the test. And as with those cruel, illogical trials of the past, the truth we were trying to find out was some inner truth of his character, and the lake and the car between them were our only means of knowing.

Had he lost his nerve? Was there some fear that held him back? Did he really want to go through with the attempt, or was there something from his past making it impossible for him ever to achieve this record he had suffered so much for already?

At the camp the trial was adjourned as the car was jacked up and hosed and wheeled back to the brown creosotesmelling hangar for another night, and Campbell took a car back to Muloorina with his wife. She drove. He slept almost all the way.

There was a fog of tobacco, an air of bitterness and disbelief and tension in the canteen at the army camp when the meeting was held that night to discuss the latest hold-up to the program. The lighting was very bright. Benches had been set in a horseshoe around the trestle table where Campbell was sitting alone in the glare of the 150-watt bulbs that had been strung just above his head between the tent poles. He looked paler than usual. He tried lighting a cigarette but his lighter would not work, and when no one seemed to notice or offer him a light he slipped the cigarette back into the packet.

The lighting and the close-packed benches and the silence that fell the moment Campbell had entered marked this meeting off immediately from all the other interminable get-togethers and press conferences preceding it. Most of the other meetings had been held to provide something for us to do, and to reassure us that things were happening and that we were not left out. Tonight's meeting was different.

It looked like a field tribunal improvised to get the truth in a hurry, and from the moment he spoke Campbell had reacted awkwardly to it, speaking anxiously, a shade too loudly, as he usually did at the prospect of criticism he could not cope with.

The strangest thing about that meeting was the silence. Perhaps there were people there who believed Campbell really had felt the vibrations. Norris probably did. He was sitting to the left, looking tired and worried and holding a file of papers that he never opened. Leo Villa would have believed him, too, for belief in Campbell was part of his life. But apart from them there can have been no one that night who did not have his doubts.

"Well, gentlemen, I'm pretty confident about what happened this afternoon," began Campbell with sad jauntiness. "The suspension is inoperative. The precise cause has yet to be discovered, but I suspect the injection of emulsified salt at high speeds."

He paused as if waiting to be challenged, but no one spoke. The moment affected Mustard more than anyone else in the

112

room. If Campbell really was cracking now, if these vibrations of his were only one more delayed symptom of his brain
injury, a trick of a battered mind to warn him off the speed at
which he had crashed at Utah, it would be Mustard's turn
to take over. As reserve driver he would have to drive Bluebird and show that he at least had the courage to get the
record. He, not Campbell, might become holder of the world
land speed record.

But it was a difficult position for him that night. It was one
thing to suspect that Campbell was suffering from nervous
hallucinations. It was another to prove it so conclusively that
Campbell, most jealous and obstinate of men, would be
forced to give up this car he had worked ten years to complete. So no one spoke and Campbell was free to continue.

"We think that the terrible conditions have begun to affect
the car at last. That the wet salt has been forced up into the
body and has worked its way into the suspension. This means
that the only thing we can do is to change the suspension
units. This is a fairly complex operation and will take Leo
Villa and his boys three days of solid work. After that I will
be ready to run immediately. Believe me, gentlemen, no one
regrets further delay at this point more than I do, but there
is absolutely no alternative. Has anyone any questions?"

It was Wally Parr who spoke then, quietly, reasonably, re-
minding us all that for readers of newspapers, for anyone
away from our tight, in-bred little group at Lake Eyre, what
mattered was fact rather than belief or prejudice or emotion.

"What about Bluebird's recorder, Donald? Surely it was
running? What did it show of these vibrations you say you
felt?"

"There you've got me, Wally," replied Campbell. "That's
the very devil of it. We find we have perfect recordings for
this morning's first two attempts, but for the one where the
vibrations started the recorder had run out of film."

"So you have no recording," said Parr, putting away his pencil.

"So we have no recording."

Once more it was the silence inside the tent that must have told Campbell what everyone was thinking. He and Mustard were staring directly at each other now—Campbell, his mouth pursed in anger, his eyes pale and very bright; Mustard, solemn, restrained.

"If anyone thinks that these vibrations were a figment of my imagination," Campbell said, still looking at Mustard and growling the words out like the challenge they were, "they might be in a better position to judge such things if they had had some experience of the sort of speed at which I encountered them."

On this note of bitterness the meeting at the army camp ended.

CHAPTER NINE

IT was very dark outside the tent. There were no stars and the night air was cold, colder than any night since we reached Lake Eyre.

"It's midwinter here now. It'll soon be June," said the cameraman from the film unit as we walked back to the homestead. He was a large, red-faced man from Brisbane who had lived on the outback many years.

"Whatever he's up to he'll have to get a move on. There's rain on the way. I can smell rain. So can the flies. Have you seen how they've been coming indoors all day, and how the ants have been digging? It's always a sign. The rain's on its way."

The wind had increased, shifted to the northeast, the rain quarter, and was humming in the big aerial over the homestead like raiding airplanes.

Leo Villa must have driven straight back from the meeting, for he was already in the kitchen drinking his last cup of tea before turning in. Behind him were the big white refrigerator, the green painted cupboard around the rainwater tank, the crates of beer, cartons of green beans, canned asparagus, Golden Shred, Johnnie Walker whisky. A large aluminum kettle was hissing somnolently on the black and silver cooking range. As Villa heaped his three spoonfuls of sugar into his blue and white cup, the glare of the kitchen light showed up the neatly cropped silver hair above his ears. He yawned, tasted the tea, and looked very much at home.

"Worried?" he said. "By this evening's caper? If you let things like that worry you, you'll never get very far in this game. I always tell Donald he takes too much notice of people —this man Mustard, for instance.

"Now Donald's old man was different. Totally different. You should have seen how he handled the press. None of this having them around all the time, waiting to pick up any little thing that goes wrong. That wasn't Sir Malcolm. He'd have the press along when he was due to run—give them a drink, show them the car, answer any questions they'd got, very polite, very firm—then he'd look at his watch and say, 'Well, gentlemen, if you will excuse us now I'm sure you'll understand we've work to do.' And that'd be that. Very much the gentleman, Sir Malcolm. And I must say, the press used to know their place in those days."

Leo Villa was a mechanic of the old school and this was his strength. For him the only real problems were mechanical ones. He had no doubts about Campbell, and if he said there were vibrations it was his job to find the cause.

"I said I'd see Donald through this record," he said as he poured himself some more tea. "After this I think I'll call it a day. Perhaps a bungalow in Devon. I'm sixty-five next birthday, and while I'm getting older the cars aren't getting any simpler.

"Take this present spot of nonsense. There's the whole suspension to strip down. Terrible job. It's hard to explain but the suspension works on big pneumatic legs. There's one for each wheel. Wonderful idea, I'm not saying it isn't, but it's a bitch of a thing to work on and we've got to strip down the entire wheel assembly to reach them. That's what'll take the time."

As he spoke the difference between him and Ken Norris became clearer than it had ever been—Norris the designer, the mathematician, with his graphs and his neat calculations, working out the problems of a world record as a complex application of aerodynamics, Villa preparing to solve the trouble with his hands, with three days' hard work and the experience of forty years behind him.

"As a piece of design the car is a masterpiece. But it's a devil to work on. If you'd just wanted a car to get the record you could have had something far simpler, but this thing's a laboratory on wheels. That gives you an awful lot that can go wrong, and if it does there's no latitude on anything. Everything in this car's calculated to a degree."

He might have said more, but Campbell came in.

"Well, Unc. So there you are. I might have known." He was smoking a large Havana cigar. The wind had blown his hair across his forehead. He smiled at Villa, put his hand on his shoulder, and sat down beside him. Suddenly he looked very young, Villa very old.

"You know there's definitely rain on the way, Unc." He smiled at Villa apologetically as if the rain, like everything else, was possibly his fault. "You understand what that'll mean, don't you?"

Villa looked down at his cup, shrugged his shoulders almost imperceptibly, and in the silence that followed you could hear the ticking of the big Japanese kitchen clock, the whisper of steam from the kettle on the range. When Campbell spoke at last he was no longer smiling. It was a very different Campbell from the man who had faced Andrew Mustard at the meeting.

"Unc, up at that meeting tonight, I was right, wasn't I? I mean, there could have been no question of going on until we had found out what was really wrong?"

" 'Course not, Skipper. It'd have been madness."

"Well, the whole thing's come to that now. But you know I was right, don't you?"

The appeal for Villa's approval surprised me, but the old

117

man seemed to find nothing odd in it and simply looked at Campbell and said, "Don't worry, Donald. We'll sort out whatever there is that needs looking at, and we'll start on that suspension first thing tomorrow morning. My alarm's set for 5:30."

"Well, you must get your sleep then, Unc, and take it as easy as you can. Let the others do the heavy work. Nothing's worth hurting yourself over."

"You know," he went on when Villa had collected his towel and his toothbrush and his soap dish and gone off toward the bathroom, "I wasn't joking about the car today. Believe me, I wasn't joking at all. When I hit those vibrations around 300 it was like being on a vibro-massage machine going full pelt, and I've really no idea how I kept control of the car. It was within a bee's whisker of going right off the track. I had it happen to me once, and believe you me, once in a lifetime's quite enough for that sort of experience."

It was as if he was talking now to convince himself, and the more he talked about the crash at Utah, the more doubts one had, the more substance he seemed to give to all the old rumors about his brain damage that had started spreading around the camp again. Where is the line dividing caution from cowardice? And suppose, just suppose, Campbell really was sick and the vibrations were the product of his sickness. How could you tell?

He must have known what I was thinking, for he smiled wearily and stubbed out the remains of his cigar and said, "I know what everyone's saying, John. I'm not such a fool as some people seem to think, and I know that Mr. Mustard would get in that cockpit tomorrow morning if I'd let him. It's what he's always wanted. I don't doubt his courage, whatever some people say about mine. No, he'd put his foot down as I once put my foot down and—bingo."

He spread his hands.

118

"I don't care overmuch what Mr. Andrew Mustard does to himself at this stage of the game, but I do care about the car. It would grieve me to see nine years' work going down the drain."

That evening everyone at Muloorina had his own views on Campbell's predicament, and the arguments went on until the last lights flickered in the army camp and the beer was exhausted and the dogs stopped barking along the creek. Some sided with Campbell. Others felt that the evening's meeting had been the equivalent of a declaration of war, and that the only question left now was how Campbell could be forced to allow his reserve driver to take over and get the record before the rains came.

Mustard himself was more reasonable. He is a man of some dignity. He was wearing his blue blazer and his flannel trousers and a white shirt. He had brushed his hair, and when he spoke he did so with the restraint and authority of an heir apparent during the final lunacy of an ailing king.

He received visitors in his trailer, a very snug, very orderly trailer with everything in its place: the telephone on the table, the bottle of Haig for guests, the neat pile of books and reports on Lake Eyre and on Bluebird, the files and notebooks and photograph albums, the map of the lake with the marks he had made from the aerial surveys. It was like a battle tent, with the engaged neatness of the headquarters of a front-line commander.

"It's quite simple. I believe Campbell is scared," he said, "and when a man's as scared as he is, the slightest trouble gets magnified out of all proportion."

"You've said all this to his face?" asked a commentator on assignment to the Australian Broadcasting Corporation. He was a large, bald man who had arrived only that day and seemed slightly appalled at what he had wandered into.

"Of course I've told him. I told him the other evening and I gave him an ultimatum. I said that either he got on with the job within a week, or I would call a press conference to announce publicly that if he wasn't willing to go for the record, there were at least three people who were."

"And you stick to that?" said the commentator slowly.

"Of course I do. Campbell is a man with a psychological block. He's no longer the same man who got the records in the boat. The closer he gets to the speed he crashed at, the more difficult it becomes for him to drive the car. I think the time has come for us to make sure that he does drive, or if he won't, that he gets out and lets someone else get on with it."

"So you doubt these vibrations Campbell says he felt this afternoon?" asked the commentator.

"It's not a question of doubting them. Of course you get vibrations in a car going at that speed. Hell, man, you must expect some discomfort. All I know is that if you want a world record you must go through the hazards that are necessary to obtain it. You don't cry off at every minor setback."

Watching him talk it was impossible to doubt his sincerity. There was no question of Andrew Mustard's passionate anxiety that Bluebird should get the record. There was no question of his own willingness to accept the risks this involved. And granted his assessment of Campbell's character and the state of his mind, there was no question that he was right.

But if he were wrong about Campbell?

"You'd be willing to drive the car as it is on that track, Andrew?" the commentator asked earnestly. "You'd be willing to drive it yourself?"

"Tomorrow, sir. A lot of people have put a lot of money

120

into this Bluebird project and I think they should start getting their money's worth."

The atmosphere at Muloorina changed now. There was a closeness in the air, a scrupulous politeness between the homestead and the army camp. For the first time people began to watch what they said, and all the extravagant, noisy arguments that had gone on in the beer tent at night were over. Suspicion started. It was a bad time.

Leo Villa was working all day at the lake on Bluebird's suspension, and a second shift had been organized under Tom Scrimshire to carry on during the night. Whatever the outcome between Campbell and Mustard, Bluebird had to be ready now as soon as possible.

Then even this seemed pointless, for on the second night of the overhaul the rain finally arrived as the red-faced cameraman had said it would—heavy spots of rain from the harsh black clouds that had been streaming above us all day from the north. It arrived at 9:15, spasmodically at first, like isolated bullets being fired against the tin roof of the verandah, then rattling with a sudden crescendo as the storm broke.

When it eased off a little I stood at the door of the homestead, and as I smelled for the first time the unforgettable faint smell of wet salt-bush blowing from the outback, the rain seemed a godsend. It would kill the record bid stone dead, and I could feel nothing but relief that this bitter tournament would now be over.

I did not want to see Campbell destroy himself. I did not want to see Mustard do it, either. And during the last few days the car seemed to have grown out of hand, to have turned into a monstrous presence on its dead lake, a sort of minotaur waiting for its sacrifices and bringing out the self-

121

ishness and the fear and the bitterness of everyone who believed in it.

But now the attempt would have to be abandoned and we could leave Lake Eyre and return to sanity.

The storm had subsided. It was fresh and cool, and I walked across from the homestead to the post office trailer to inquire if any aircraft were expected to make the journey down to Adelaide during the next few days.

Parr had just sent his copy through to his office in Sydney and was standing in the lighted doorway. He wore his hat and watched the rain with an expression of bleak satisfaction.

"So we'll never know the answer, will we?" he said. "We'll never know who was right, Donald Campbell or Andrew Mustard."

"Does it matter?" I said.

"Yes, it does matter. I hate people giving me puzzles and then not letting me find out the answer."

He stepped down from the trailer and strolled with me through the rain.

"What I find so satisfactory about literature is that you usually get an answer of sorts in the end. No writer would ever leave his characters in the state the people here are in."

He stopped and looked across at the homestead. All the lights were on, and a car had just drawn up. The engine was still running and the headlights were on, throwing tapering shafts of yellow light through the rain. Then the doors of the homestead opened, car doors slammed, and the engine and the headlights were extinguished.

"That's Campbell now," he said, "just arrived back from the lake to tell everyone it's all over."

We watched silently for a moment, both trying to imagine what was going on inside the homestead now that Campbell was there. Then the rain increased and we started to walk toward Parr's hut.

"Do you really know the man at all?" he said. "Do you know why he's in the record game, or the real truth about his father, or about that crash in Utah? Have you even made up your mind yet about those vibrations of his? I haven't. I can't even make up my mind whether he's a nut case or the one really sane man in the place."

"Unless the car runs again now, you'll never know," I said. "If that's the price of knowing, I'd rather leave things as they are."

"But what about Campbell?" said Parr, pushing his hat back on his head and dabbing at his forehead with his handkerchief. "D'you think that's what he feels? Perhaps he'd like to know the answers, too."

By now it was hard to tell exactly what Campbell did feel. He looked defeated, gray-faced, as he sat in the kitchen with Ken Norris. But appearances alone were no answer to the sort of questions Parr had asked. The rain was still on his face and his hair was straggled down his forehead.

Elliot Price came in.

"Well, you've got your rain, Elliot," said Campbell flatly. "You can have your extra sheep now. You've got the feed you needed for the next twelve months. You and the sheep have won."

"Don't you be so sure, Donald. I've a hunch it won't rain all that much on the lake this time. Oftentimes it rains on the homestead hard but not on the lake. I'll bet you a pound, Don—a pound sterling if you like—that you don't have twenty points of rain on the lake during this twenty-four hours. And the bit of rain you have had will be just what you need to bind the surface of the salt together."

He stood for a moment looking at Campbell. He had done his best and Campbell, appreciating this, smiled at him weakly and raised his hand.

123

"Okay, Elliot, you old rogue. A pound it is. But this is one bet you can't win."

"You never know, Don," replied Price as he closed the door behind him.

"Ken," Campbell said when the old man was gone, "I should never have come to this bloody place. Never." He poured himself some whisky, a drink he almost never took. "It was a total error of judgment from the very beginning. Nothing, not one damn thing has gone right since I first saw the place four years ago."

He seemed to hunch forward over the table as he spoke, and the words came in a weary, detached voice.

"Thank our lucky stars, I suppose, that we've still got the old boat. She's a bit ancient now, but she's good for another crack at the water record. But there's absolutely no point in going on here with the car, is there? This rain's finished everything."

Norris nodded but said nothing, and his silence was more impressive than if he had spoken. After Campbell, he and his firm had more to lose from the decision to abandon the attempt than anyone. Bluebird might belong to Campbell, but the design had come from Norris and his brother and he had lived with it for many years. Now, through no fault of his, it would end up as one more design that never quite achieved its purpose.

Campbell must have realized this. "Of course I'll hang on to the car, Ken," he said. "Perhaps we'll even be able to have a go with it on some other track one day. Next year, for that matter. No reason why we shouldn't. But not here," he said bitterly, "never again here."

But as it turned out, Elliot Price was to win his bet. By some freak of the weather the storm veered away from the lake

124

and only three points of rain, three hundredths of an inch, actually fell on the track—enough to delay things yet again, to make the surface just that much more treacherous, but not enough to finish everything once and for all. And when Leo Villa had finished the overhaul at the end of the third day, he said he could find nothing that really accounted for the vibrations.

The following evening Parr stopped Norris on the verandah after dinner, and again asked if there was any news on the vibrations.

"No, we're not sure, although I've an idea of my own what it is."

"And what's that?"

"I'd rather keep it to myself until after tomorrow morning's run. I could easily be wrong. At any rate, Leo seems to have ruled out anything being wrong with the car."

"And you've no doubt at all that Campbell really did feel these vibrations of his."

"No doubt at all."

"But aren't you asking him, then, to do something extremely dangerous tomorrow morning if he drives into the vibration belt again?"

"Of course. This whole business is extremely dangerous. Not everybody seems to appreciate it, though."

"And does he really understand the risk he's taking?"

"He understands, all right. But if he's going to get the record we've got to find out what caused the trouble first, and if you've any ideas how we can do that without running Bluebird at 300 tomorrow morning, I'd be very glad to hear them."

CHAPTER TEN

SO it was that on the morning of Wednesday, May 27th, Campbell—gray-faced, hunch-shouldered, with two cups of coffee and a helping of Corn Flakes in his stomach—drove down to Lake Eyre at 6:15 for his next speed trials. Much was at stake. The truth about the vibrations, for one thing; the outcome of his battle with Andrew Mustard, for another; the whole question of his mental condition, for yet another.

The night before he had promised publicly (a thing he always disliked doing) that he intended to achieve "several runs around the 300-mile-an-hour mark to give Ken Norris and the engineers the readings they need before we can proceed to higher speeds."

This time the film cassettes on Bluebird's recorder had been checked and rechecked. The time-keepers would be there. There would be no misunderstandings.

All this showed on Campbell's face as he waited by the hangar while the mechanics made their last adjustments to Bluebird on that gray morning. They took no longer than usual, but now each stage in the final preparations seemed one more attempt to prolong his ordeal.

The controls were checked: the air pressure for his pneumatic brakes, the compressed air he breathed in the cockpit for the three or four minutes of the run, the valve controlling the percentage of power from the turbine.

"There's a wind of three knots, southeast, Don," shouted Carl Noble. "Shouldn't worry you."

"We've given you sixty percent power on the turbine," said Norris. "That'll be more than enough. Take her up steadily to 300, then see what happens. If you get the vibrations hold her as long as you can before bringing her down. If not, take her on up."

Campbell nodded. The check-through was nearly over, and Tonia was waiting near the car with the blue bag, when Andrew Mustard arrived from inspecting the track in his red racing car. He wore a clean pair of white overalls with his name on the back.

"Morning, Andy, old boy. Everything all right?" said Campbell.

Mustard took off his sunglasses and smiled. "Good morning, Donald. At the moment the track is perfect. We've been over the surface once more this morning with the drags, and you have twelve and three-quarter miles. I believe it's as smooth now as you'll ever get it. Whatever was causing those vibrations of yours, I don't think you'll find it's the track."

"Let's just hope not, Andy. Let's hope not."

As usual before a run, Campbell seemed a solitary, strangely lonely figure. Perhaps it was the imminent possibility of death that isolated him from the rest of us. The risk he was about to take made conversation difficult, as I realized when I found myself standing next to him.

"You know," he said suddenly, "I'd give almost anything to be a thousand miles away from here at the moment." He looked down at the salt and neither of us spoke. The mechanics had nearly finished now, and Tonia was waiting by the cockpit.

"It's not so much the business of being afraid," he said,

"although fear's the one thing you never get used to. You can't train yourself to endure fear as you might endure hunger. Fear's always as bad, every time. But it's not that that worries me, it's just the strain of this whole damn business. I'm not sure I can take it much longer or that I even *want* to take it much longer."

"Ready now, Skipper?" shouted Leo Villa from the front of the car.

"Coming, Unc, coming," Campbell said quietly, but as we started walking toward the car he went on. "You see, if you're going to take a record in a machine like this you really have to want it. You have to want it with your whole being just as you have to want a woman if you're going to make her properly. With this record, I've reached the point where I'm not sure that I want to make it any more."

"Compressor on. Ready when you are," shouted Carl Noble.

"She's all yours, Skipper," said Villa, unfastening the safety cable that held open the cockpit canopy.

"The trouble is," said Campbell as he untied the laces of his suede desert boots, "there's only a certain amount the old nervous system can stand and I reckon I've just about got there."

During the first run that morning I watched Norris and Villa. They were together in the car in which we followed Bluebird along the track. The Valiant was doing over 90, and as they squinted through the windshield along the glaring white track ahead, it must have been very like that other 90-mile-an-hour dash they made together four years before. I remembered the words from Norris' report when that dash was over. "We were doing a good 90 mph. . . . The past kept imposing itself with endless accusations. You should have done this and that and that! ! !"

But whatever self-accusations Norris had now, he was keeping to himself. So was Leo Villa. They sat quite still,

128

their faces like masks, and it was not until we had reached the far end of the track and the Valiant had skidded to a halt that their anxiety showed for just a moment as they leaped from the car and rushed across to Campbell.

He looked battered and even worse than before the run.

"Well, the vibrations are still there," he said. "Hit me just past 310."

"Bad as ever?" asked Villa.

"Not quite, but I still thought I was going to get my eyes shaken out of my head."

Instead of getting out of the car as he usually did, Campbell sat where he was, and gradually a crowd collected as the rest of the cars arrived. Once again his weird ability to impose his mood on the people around him began to show itself. Because he was quiet, everyone else was, too. Voices were lowered.

"Was it bad, darling?" Tonia asked, leaning over the edge of the car.

He nodded.

"You'd think it was a funeral," said one of the cameramen.

"That's just what it is," murmured Wally Parr beneath his breath. "But I'm interested in Ken Norris. I've an idea that if anyone knows the answer to all this, he does."

While Parr was speaking, Norris had left the side of the cockpit and walked slowly toward the back of the car. There was no one else there, and we watched him as he bent down by one of the rear wheels and carefully ran his finger round the inside of the rim. Then he walked to the other side of the car and did the same.

Whatever he had found, he seemed to be keeping to himself. We watched him open his brown folder, scribble some figures in pencil, scratch his head, and then walk away.

"I'd like to know just what he's up to," said Parr. "Let's go and look at those wheels for ourselves."

Bluebird's wheels are enormous. The tires are completely smooth, made up of layer upon layer of rayon and wafer-thin rubber, and the rim of the wheel is a couple of inches deep. Parr bent down and ran his thumb along the bottom of the rim as we had seen Norris doing.

"Very interesting," he said. "Just look at that." When he held out his thumb I saw that it was covered with something thick and white like toothpaste.

"You'd hardly believe it, would you," he said.

"What is it?"

"Salt, I suppose. With the wet on the surface of the track it must be getting thrown up by the speed of the wheels and then packing against the rims. It's quite thick."

We walked toward the front of the car where the inquest on the run was still in progress. Andrew Mustard was there now and most of the engineers. Leo Villa was explaining why the source of the vibrations could not lie in the suspension.

"Are you sure that the recorder was operating that time?" asked Mustard. But nobody answered, and nobody seemed to know whether Campbell would make another run now or not.

"Andrew," said Norris suddenly. "I think we should change the wheels."

Mustard was the official Dunlop representative under the arrangement Campbell had with the company. He was responsible to Campbell, but the wheels and tires that Dunlop had developed specially for the car remained their property.

"Certainly, Ken, if you think it can help, although all the wheels have been checked for balance and accuracy countless times, as you know."

"I know. But I'd like to see what happens if we change them all the same."

So the wheels were changed; quite quickly in fact, for Blue-

130

bird could raise itself on four pneumatic rams that came sliding from beneath its belly at the touch of a button. These rams were one of Campbell's own ideas, which Norris had skillfully incorporated into the design. Leo Villa's team was trained to perform the entire operation at full speed in readiness for the actual record bid when, as a matter of course, the wheels would be switched between the first and second runs.

The four panels at the side of the car were lifted off, exposing the great convex silver discs of the wheels. The rams came down, and silently, effortlessly, Bluebird raised herself a further two inches off the ground. The fresh wheels were pushed forward on small, yellow tubular steel trolleys, and when the hub bolts had been undone and the old wheels removed, the new ones were lifted carefully into place and bolted home. The whole operation took something less than ten minutes. Then Bluebird gently lowered itself again, and the rams slid back into its body.

"Now, Andrew," said Norris, "would you make sure that the rims have been wiped absolutely clear of all trace of salt?"

"But they are clean. They're fresh wheels."

"Good," said Norris, and the wheel panels were fixed back into position.

Campbell started putting on his helmet once more, and Leo Villa stood by the cockpit talking earnestly.

"Looks as if we are having another run after all," said Parr. "This is going to be important. Let's go right up the track so we see what happens when he gets to the other end."

So we took one of the trucks and drove off along the service road that ran along the length of the main track, passing the big red marker at the start of the measured mile and the trailer with the slender aluminum aerial where the timekeepers kept their equipment. We waited ten minutes until

Bluebird had flashed by with the unearthly sound of its acceleration, half whine, half roar. It appeared faster than we had seen it before.

"Let's find out what's happened," said Parr. He started the engine and we raced off in pursuit. But on the way the gray Valiant passed us with Norris and Villa aboard, and we reached Bluebird in time to see Campbell handing the crash helmet to Norris and levering himself out of the cockpit. He was smiling faintly to himself but making no attempt to talk.

"Well, Skipper," said Villa anxiously, "how was that one?"

"Not so bad, Unc," Campbell said softly. "Not so bad."

"What sort of speed?"

"Something just over 300."

"And the vibrations?" asked Norris. "Did you feel them again?"

"No, Ken. Not a sign. She behaved beautifully."

Norris' trailer at Muloorina had been parked at the back of the homestead next door to the bungalow where one of Elliot's daughters lived with her family. And it was in this trailer that he spent almost the rest of that day working on the film that had come out of Bluebird's recorder. Ken Reaks and Carl Noble helped him develop it and festoon it across the trailer to dry. When I called on them just after 5:00, Ken Reaks was setting up the small film projector used for examining the film, a frame at a time.

"So he *was* right about the vibrations," I said.

"Sure," Norris said. "He was right all along, and he was even right at the very beginning when he diagnosed wheel unbalance. The film shows it quite clearly. As soon as old Reaks has got his projector working I'll let you see for yourself. The vibrations were very bad. He was lucky to get away with it."

132

"But why did they vanish on the final run this morning? Was there something wrong with the first set of wheels?"

"No, the wheels themselves were perfectly all right. All that was happening was that over several runs the wet salt had been drying unevenly inside the rims and making them just a fraction out of balance. I suspected wheel trouble too when Don complained of the vibrations, but Andrew was so insistent that they were all perfectly balanced. I should have thought of the salt drying unevenly before. It was only this morning that I guessed it."

"What I still don't understand, Ken, is how a few spoonfuls of salt could make all that difference," said Reaks. Reaks is a small, jolly man with bright blue eyes and a very large mustache. He has been supervising Campbell's instrumentation since the days of his record bids with the boat on Coniston Water.

"Well, at the speed those wheels travel, a couple of ounces out of balance would make all the difference," replied Norris. "If you've got the projector working now I'll show you what two ounces of salt can do."

The projector was plugged in, and threw a bright yellow rectangle a yard wide on the far wall of the trailer.

"Here," said Norris, feeding the first strip of film through the machine. "At this point Bluebird's traveling at around 120. You see the lines from all four suspensions are pretty straight. The only fluctuation comes from one or two bumps along the track. Nothing to worry about at that speed. The top black line is the steering movement. You see it's absolutely straight."

He pushed his hair back, and leaned over to feed the film on.

"Here he is just past the second-mile mark, doing about 240." He traced the bottom suspension line across the screen with his finger. "He was taking her up very steadily, and you

133

can see there's still nothing much to worry about. Ideally, of course, you'd like all the lines to be straight, but these variations are all right. But here," he said as he wound more film on, "here's where the real trouble begins. At about 220, three and a half miles down the track."

From the picture on the wall it looked as if the recorder had suddenly developed St. Vitus dance, for each of the black lines for the suspension had become jagged and even the steering line fluctuated sharply.

"It must have been a terrible job to keep her on the track at all," he said, pointing to the top line. "You can see what the vibrations were doing to the steering."

"But it'll be all right now," said Reaks.

"Sure," said Norris, "it'll be all right now."

And it was all right—more than all right. On the surface, at any rate. The following morning Campbell drove again and went his fastest yet, and for the first time since he had been at Lake Eyre the record seemed within reach.

It was a great moment when the run was over. He sat on the back of the cockpit, grinning as he took off his crash helmet, and winked at Ken Norris.

"She's not an easy car to drive, but she goes. I'll say that for you, Ken. This car of yours is a goer."

Just as we had shared in all the previous failures, so now success was here for everyone. Norris beamed, giving Campbell his shy smile.

"Well, Don. You can't have everything. Any vibrations that time?"

"No. Nothing like we had before."

"What speed d'you think, Skipper?" asked Villa proudly.

"Off the record, Unc, I'd say 345, but I may be right up the wall."

He changed from the blue sneakers to the suede desert boots, slid down onto the salt, and kissed Tonia on both

134

cheeks. They looked happy and successful. And when the official speed from the time-keepers came over the radio— 352 miles an hour through the measured mile—Campbell kissed his wife again.

As they were walking away I heard Parr's voice from the radio on the Morris 1100 repeating the news back to Muloo-rina for transmission over to the Australian Associated Press office in Adelaide.

The loudspeakers made his voice sound high pitched and not quite human. ". . . Three-five-two miles an hour officially timed. The nearest to Campbell's highest speed on land when he crashed four years ago at Utah at three-six-zero."

There was a very short meeting that night and the atmosphere was discreet. There was no sign of excitement, even when Campbell announced that after his run that day he had telephoned Mr. Don Thompson, secretary of the Club of Australian Motor Sports, requesting that official stewards be sent to Lake Eyre as soon as possible.

There were no congratulations, no spontaneous admissions of error. Campbell looked tired and clearly had no great wish to stay talking for long.

"So you could get the record on Saturday, Don," a voice said.

Campbell smiled. "Let us not be premature, gentlemen."

CHAPTER ELEVEN

IT WAS as Campbell left the meeting that Norris stopped him. "Don, I'm worried. Something rather dreadful's happened. Just had a telephone call from Marjorie. The baby's coming earlier than we expected. I'm desperately worried. If anything happened and I wasn't there, I'd never forgive myself."

"But I thought it was the second week in June the baby was due."

"So did we. Marjorie wouldn't say much on the phone but I'm afraid something might have gone wrong."

"Well, there's no question about it, then. You must get back to England right away."

"I'm sorry about it, Don. It's the worst possible moment for this to happen, but I'm worried stiff about them at home."

"Of course, I understand. Your family's got to come first. I'll fly you down to Adelaide first thing tomorrow morning; it'll do me good to get away from here for a day. But what about analyzing the recordings from the last runs? Can you manage that before you go?"

"I'll stay up tonight and finish them. The car seems to be behaving perfectly now, and I can't see that any further adjustments will be needed, but if anything does crop up after I've left, Carl Noble can work out the mathematics as well as I can."

"No one knows the car as you do, Ken. We shall miss you. Believe me, we'll miss you."

Campbell put his hand on his shoulder and the two of them walked to the blue Humber in which Campbell had driven to the meeting.

"One thing we might do, Ken," he said. "When we get back to the homestead, why not telephone through to your doctor. With a baby on the way a lot of things can get exaggerated over twelve thousand miles, and he might be able to set your mind at rest a little."

The operator at Adelaide had reported an hour's delay on all calls to London, and Norris, looking really worried for the first time since he reached Lake Eyre, had gone back to the trailer to work on his analysis until the telephone rang. Campbell waited, too. He settled himself into the blue deck chair on the verandah and gloomily lit a large cigar.

"I don't like it," he said. "I don't like any of it. I'm fetching the stewards up now because I've got to, but we're not really ready for the record yet, not by a long chalk. I'm not even going to get those fifteen runs I wanted."

He puffed hard at the cigar. Large, white-bellied moths were clinging to the mosquito wire behind his head.

"I've got to make an attempt within the next few days. I can't afford the expense of the thing dragging on much longer, and in a week most of the engineers will have to get back to their firms in England. The weather's breaking. I don't know why. According to statistics, December should be the wettest month and the wind doesn't usually come until July. Now there's this business with Ken," he said. "It really is as though something's against me."

He put his left hand behind his neck and pushed his head back as far as it would go.

"Hell, it's stiff," he said. He went on smoking, and the

moths clambered awkwardly up toward the light. Occasionally one would lose its grip and slither down the wire.

"There was only one occasion when I saw my father afraid. I've never forgotten it. That was at Utah, too—funny the way our paths keep crossing—Utah in 1935. He was there with his new car, 2500 horsepower. She was to be his last Bluebird car, and he'd set his heart on being the first man to travel at over 300 on land. He took me with him to Salt Lake City. I was at Uppingham still. I was pretty sick of school, and it was the greatest treat of my life, for I really worshipped the old man, you know.

"I was there when he made his first run through the measured mile on the record bid, and something went wrong. When Leo and I reached Bluebird after the run, one of the front tires was burning and he was standing by the car looking deathly pale."

Campbell had told me the story some time before, but he must have forgotten, for the whole experience was a key passage in his career, and as he went on I was fascinated to see how he was repeating himself word for word.

"I said, 'What happened, Dad?'

" 'Near side front tire burst when I had her going at 304,' he replied. But that wasn't all. Exhaust fumes had been coming into the cockpit and he'd nearly passed out. He looked very grim. 'Will the run back be all right, Dad?' I asked. 'Have to be, boy. Have to be.' That was all he said. When the tire was changed he climbed back into the cockpit and got the record. That's the sort of man he was."

Campbell paused and looked up. "You know, I've never forgotten the way he looked at me as he said those words. And I never quite managed to ask him what he was thinking. But now I'm in the game myself I know. He thought he'd had it."

The telephone rang, and Norris came from the trailer to

138

take the call in the Prices' sitting room. Campbell, silent now, stayed on in the deck chair, finishing the cigar.

At last the door opened and Norris came out. He looked at Campbell and smiled a little.

"Well, Ken," said Campbell, "what's the verdict?"

"The specialist says now that it definitely won't be until the weekend. Marjorie's comfortable and I'm to phone again tomorrow morning. It looks as though I've a day or two more here, at any rate."

"Thanks, Ken. Perhaps there is a chance after all."

"Sit perfectly still, hands by your sides, and breathe in and out deeply as fast as you can like this."

The small man in the combat uniform of a RAAF flight lieutenant was breathing with quite startling power and rapidity, and Campbell, sitting beside him on a brown kitchen chair, began doing the same.

It was the next evening and we were at the homestead. The stewards were due by charter plane from Melbourne sometime the following morning. Ken Norris had been told by his doctor that the immediate anxiety for his wife was over. And since the news of the stewards' arrival had leaked out, a whole crop of visitors was expected for the weekend. Campbell had spent the day visiting the lake, and now after dinner he had asked the newly arrived medical officer, Dr. Denis Burke, over for a drink.

Burke, an Adelaide general practitioner, was on the Air Force reserve and had been sent to Lake Eyre as medical officer. We discovered that evening that he had pronounced views of his own on the subject of aviation medicine—views that Campbell was later to learn did not always coincide with the official Air Force policy.

He was a powerful talker, with earnest brown eyes and a

139

strong Irish jaw, and he and Campbell found a subject of immediate mutual interest in the causes of the crash at Utah. Campbell described to him the symptoms of his loss of control before the crash.

"Sounds like a perfectly straightforward case of hyperventilation," said Burke. "The carbon dioxide level in the blood gets lowered dangerously through overbreathing. In your case the oxygen you inhaled would have been the primary factor. We often get cases of this with pilots under stress. Used to be a serious cause of unexplained accidents until we learned what was happening. Causes the pilot to lose all sense of judgment and most of his skill. Acute cases of hyperventilation seem to have no sense of danger or personal involvement with what they're doing."

Burke spoke with the assured enthusiasm doctors sometimes show when embarked upon their favorite theories, but Campbell had already discussed hyperventilation with experts in England and America.

"Of course, in my case, it was the fact of inhaling pure oxygen at sea level that caused the crash," he said.

"Probably," replied Burke, "but that needn't have been the only factor. These things vary from individual to individual, according to the personal blood chemistry. All the symptoms you had may have been due simply to overbreathing."

"You mean it could happen again," said Campbell, "even though I'm no longer using oxygen?"

"Cases have been known," replied Burke, "of subjects overbreathing under stress and showing very similar symptoms to those you just described."

"For crying out loud," Campbell said.

"I've known several cases with combat pilots," added Burke, "and the American space project people have had to face the same phenomenon—overbreathing in time of high nervous

140

tension, resulting in acute lowering of the carbon dioxide level in the blood.

"It's very simple to correct. Carbon dioxide's the answer. Just a whiff. Completely restores the carbon dioxide level in the blood. You'd be surprised how swiftly the symptoms of hyperventilation vanish. Remarkable stuff, carbon dioxide. I've used it to banish symptoms of the common cold, and I've used it with effect in cases of rheumatism."

Dr. Burke sat back. His face had turned rather pink, and he regarded Campbell with every sign of satisfaction. "I think," he added, "that we should know what effect over-breathing has on you."

So the experiment began.

Campbell kept up the deep breathing for about a minute. His face was tense and grew rapidly paler; his knuckles showed white as he gripped the arms of the chair. His breathing was like that of a woman in advanced childbirth.

"Very well, Donald. How do you feel?" asked Dr. Burke in a reassuring medical voice. "Any change yet?"

"Slight tingling in the hands and feet."

"Very good. Carry on please, Donald.

"Now, Donald," he said a few seconds later. "Maintain your breathing rate, but would you mind getting up and walking round the room? Take your time."

With some uncertainty, Campbell got to his feet and, still breathing as heavily as ever, navigated his way past the green sofa, the large yellow hassock, the standard lamp, the piano, and the television set. His movements were stiff but determined, his face preoccupied. He failed to notice the small coffee table, but Dr. Burke was there to take his arm and guide him back to his chair.

"Very good, Donald, *very* good. And now I would like you to read me something from this newspaper." He gave him the front page of a recent copy of the *Adelaide Advertiser* and

Campbell started off on the lead story. In place of the customary crisp, faintly arrogant diction the words were now labored and slurred.

"Excellent. Now would you please write your name and address on this sheet of paper?"

As Campbell picked up the pen and began to write, he was clearly having to make an enormous effort. It was as if his arm were stiff and his mind drugged. And instead of the usually flamboyant signature, his writing wavered across the page like a very old man's, but he was determined to finish.

"Very well, Donald. Now stop, and breathe normally. Slowly. Slowly. That's better."

Recovery was swift. Within five minutes Campbell was back to normal and anxiously discussing his symptoms.

"I wouldn't say extreme," said Dr. Burke, "but a pronounced reaction. You remember the way you went on stubbornly trying to finish the writing? That's another symptom of hyperventilation we found in pilots. They would just go on with some pointless activity, not seeming to realize it was no use at all."

"What would you suggest in my case then, doctor?" asked Campbell.

"Well, in the first place, don't worry about it. Worry's the very worst thing you can do. But practice shallow breathing. When you're in the cockpit avoid those deep breaths you take under stress. And I think I'd better see if I can't get you some compressed carbon dioxide. You can inhale it just before a run, and it will stop any chance of hyperventilation. Best to be on the safe side."

But Tonia was worried about the idea of giving him carbon dioxide. "We're getting very near the edge now," she said. "If any man can do it he will, but there's an awful lot against him. This is his battle and he's the only one who can fight it."

Elliot Price made perhaps the best suggestion. The next

142

day after breakfast he called on Campbell and said, "Let me take you around some of my land, Don. You can bring your guns with you and do a bit of shooting. Take your mind off things."

Campbell had begun playing solitaire again. As a rule he dislikes being disturbed in a game, but Price's idea appealed to him.

"Excellent idea, Elliot, old sport. Wait while I get a couple of guns and some ammunition." He went off in the direction of the bedroom, and when he appeared on the verandah a few minutes later in his blue Ampol battle-dress jacket with a rifle over each shoulder he looked cheerful for the first time in days. His hair stuck up and his eyes sparkled. He had a truant look about him.

"Come on, Elliot, quick. Let's get out of here."

We borrowed the big gray Valiant, shabby now with dust and the salt from the lake. Campbell took great care as he piled the rifles with their gleaming blue barrels into the trunk along with the special slings and telescopes and cleaning rods and binoculars and the heavy, neat boxes of ammunition. He likes equipment, the more expensive the better. He likes radios and knives and good cameras and machine tools. He has a beautifully kept collection of firearms at his house in Surrey. The mere act of handling the guns as he placed them in the car seemed to give him pleasure.

We drove eastward from the homestead. The worn red carpet of the airstrip lay to our right. For a moment we could still see the homestead buildings behind us. They looked delicate and impracticable, like toy sheds and farms and wind pumps placed in a wilderness for some game and then forgotten. Then the car pitched forward. The homestead vanished behind a ridge and we were alone in the most ravaged landscape in the world. It was a flat gray land where every particle of life had been scorched away, leaving this inert cinder country where the only noise was the wind scouring the low, hide-colored rocks and carrying the dust for miles in long clouds going from nowhere to nowhere.

From the front seat of the Valiant, Elliot Price regarded it with satisfaction.

"Some of my best land, this, Donald," he said, pulling back his shoulders and scratching his chest. "Know how much the bastards on the Land Board charge now? Three and nine, Donald. Three and bloody ninepence a square mile."

Campbell said nothing, and as we jolted on Price began talking about the one real enthusiasm of his life—his land— pointing out the all but invisible gray scrub, the endlessly surviving small plants that could keep sheep alive even here: the copper burr, the black blue bush, the marsh salt bush— "good feed for the sheep, Don, though Christ knows how they eat it."

But even here Campbell was unable to forget Lake Eyre. There was no escape, not for him at any rate, and when Price stopped talking to concentrate on the way ahead, he suddenly began telling me what a strain the last few days had been.

"It's not nerves," he said quietly, "and it's not fear, either. I know everyone gets nerves, but this is something different. It's only come on this week. It's a constant tension and I'm terrified it's going to impair my judgment. It makes me want to seize up completely. I was exhausted after that last run at 350 the other day, completely exhausted. I slept five hours straight off, and I've never done that before."

"Look, Donald," said Price, interrupting to point out a row of white wooden skeletons of trees along the horizon. "Coolibah trees. That's how they was along the Cooper the time they'd had no rain for thirty-six years. Dead as hell they looked. Then the rains come and the leaves start all over again."

144

We passed a big stained concrete water tank holding water for the sheep, pumped through iron piping from a well ten miles away, and he told us how the man who had supervised the work on the pipeline had been living at this very spot in a trailer with his young wife eighteen months earlier.

"Beautiful girl she was. Beautiful girl. And seven months gone when she had this miscarriage. Happened at night, it did, right here. And she bled to death in his arms. Then two days later the poor bastard's in Marree arranging her funeral and a kerosene refrigerator he's left on in the trailer catches light and burns the whole thing to a cinder. Look, Don, over there."

He stopped the car and pointed a hundred yards or so beyond the tank to where the scrub was blackened by an ancient blaze and there were still strips of twisted iron.

"Poor devil was in a terrible state, didn't eat a thing or stop crying for a fortnight. In two days flat he'd lost his wife, his trailer, and everything he had. Went off without a penny except what we could give him."

The story seemed to impress Campbell, and he insisted on leaving the car to inspect the place where the death and the blaze occurred. "You see the sort of country this is," he said as he turned the rusting angle iron over with his foot. "No mercy in it. A cruel land. A cruel, terrible land. Was there nothing he could do for the girl, Elliot, nothing at all?"

"No, Don. She just bled and that was an end to her."

We chose a spot nearby for our target practice, sticking tin cans on the ground at two and three hundred yards and using the hood of the car to rest the rifles. Campbell shot better than anyone but he did not speak at all.

CHAPTER TWELVE

THE first Saturday in June around 3:30 in the afternoon a thin, bony old man with white hair and bright
earnest eyes was standing on the verandah of the
homestead talking to Campbell. His shirt was stained. His
gray trousers had been intended for a stomach many sizes
larger than his. He had driven 250 miles across country from
Oodnadatta, the legendary cattle town to the north, and his
antique red Dodge truck was standing, still quivering from
the strain of the journey, in front of the house.

"Mr. Campbell?"

"Yes, sir. What can I do for you, sir?"

"Mr. Campbell. Me'n my boy've just drove over to see you
get the record. Reck'n we'll see anything if we stays around?"

"Well, sir, I can't promise anything. I would say it could
take anything up to another week. You can't rush these
things, you know."

"But me'n the boy thought we'd be seeing something this
weekend."

"Well, wait around, sir, and we'll see what we can do. It
all depends on the weather and the state of the lake. Wait
around, sir. Wait around."

And everyone else at Muloorina waited around, convinced
that if they could last out for one more weekend they would
see some action. Campbell would not say what his plans were

146

or what he was going to do. He seemed to have an almost superstitious horror now of committing himself to anything, promising anything, before he had actually done it. But however unprepared he might be for an all-out record bid, and whatever the state of the salt or the track, it had become tacitly accepted that he would have to try now or never. The circus had to begin, and from the previous evening a new audience had been arriving at Muloorina to see it.

There was something uncanny about the way new faces suddenly appeared, making this closed society we had endured so long suddenly public. That Saturday we had awoken to see tents pitched between the wattle bushes and the sand dunes around the homestead. Trailers had arrived. Four post office workers at a Friday night ball in Adelaide had taken a bet at midnight and driven nonstop, arriving dazed, dirty, and fifty pounds to the good just after 9:00 on Saturday morning. The landing strip had graduated overnight to a minor airport. By Saturday lunch time there were a dozen planes lining its western perimeter—two Aero Commanders, a maroon Cessna from South Australian Air Taxis, a yellow Aztec, a blue and white Beechcraft, a Skywaggon from Nicholas Air Charter.

Each fresh planeload gave Campbell another reason for putting his foot down that weekend. One of the planes had come all the way from Sydney with MacLeonard, the general manager of the Ampol oil company. By training MacLeonard was an accountant, a short, quiet man with a way of thrusting his hands into the pockets of his neat gabardine golf jacket and looking at you and making it clear from his very silence that he was in the habit of getting value for his money. Mason, his deputy general manager, had come on the same plane—tall, good-looking Mason, a former naval commander and still the right side of forty-five, very English and very anxious in the nicest possible way that Campbell

147

should get the record before too long. Mason had had a lot to do with Ampol's decision to back Campbell, and the company had much at stake.

Then there were the other plane visitors. There was a very tall, very silent millionaire from Melbourne with a beautiful wife who wore ski pants and a black leather coat and talked a lot. There was Florence, who had got back from Jakarta with her divorce and had flown up with champagne so that we could all celebrate her freedom and Campbell's record in one splendid party. And there were Grand Prix drivers like Lex Davison and Bib Stilwell, who had come out of interest in this car of Campbell's, which would try for the record at four times the speed at which they had made their own reputations in their Lotuses and Ferraris.

Before this weekend Campbell had been operating in private. All the rows and all the anxieties had been in a sense private rows and private anxieties. Now he was in public, officially billed for a performance he was unofficially insisting was not ready to start, and that Saturday his visitors and his well-wishers were like an audience turning up for a play while the rehearsals are still going on, while the playwright is arguing about the lines, and the principal actor is having doubts about whether he can go through with it.

"It shouldn't have happened like this," he said. "The old man wouldn't have let it happen like this. But then Father was always independent, and he was far too wise to take on anything quite like Lake Eyre. It was all so much simpler in his day and age, and the old man was always in a much stronger position than I am to say exactly when he was going to do something."

It was the contrast between the pressures on him now and the independence his father had enjoyed in his record-breaking that made his situation so galling. He felt trapped as he had not felt trapped before. All along he had been trying to

148

assert one thing—his right to run for the record when he was ready to run and not a moment before. All along he had been trying not to gamble any more than he had to. But now he was caught.

The story Elliot had told us the day before about the man with the trailer seemed to be on his mind, too. "Terrible story, but that's what can happen to you in a place like this. All in the space of a few hours. You lose everything, everything you possess. Your life is ruined. It's that sort of country. Either you beat it as Elliot has done, or it beats you."

But whatever doubts Campbell was having now about himself and the state of his nerves, he was keeping to himself, and for a man as worried as he was, his performance that afternoon, welcoming his visitors, laughing at their jokes, evading the one question they all wanted to ask him, was remarkable.

But that same afternoon he was having other discussions, too. He spent a long time with Ken Norris talking about the car and what was to be done. For Norris the situation was hardly less of a nightmare than it was for Campbell. Bluebird was his design. He was the only one who really understood it. Its behavior at high speeds was still untested, and Norris was in the position of a scientist working with insufficient data and a man's life at stake.

For the past two or three days he had been involved in his calculations, plotting the suspension readings from Bluebird's recorder onto graph paper and attempting to find out from the way the car had behaved at 300 miles an hour how she was likely to react at 400 plus. He was very neat with these sums. Each of Bluebird's runs had its separate sheet in his file, and each was analyzed and compared with the readings of what had gone before. But none of this was really enough in the freak conditions the car was having to encounter. The closer Bluebird got to 400, the farther it would get from that predictable area covered by the graphs and the equations.

It was a strange conversation the two of them had, strange because of the offhand, almost casual way the two men talked as they sat in the cramped office at the back of the homestead, with its one small shuttered window and the cream-painted deal table that one of Elliot's daughters used when she did the accounts for the sheep station. There was Norris in his maroon tee-shirt and his baggy brown trousers, a diffident, very quiet man whose mustache, like the sort of mustaches students grow, succeeded only in making him look even younger than he was; and Campbell as eager, as amiable as ever, with his double-breasted blue blazer specially put on to meet his visitors that afternoon.

No one seeing them here for the first time would have believed that they had any connection with what they were actually doing. It was as difficult to imagine Norris designing anything as complex, as beautiful, as deadly as the car Bluebird, as it was to think of the man opposite him getting ready to kill himself in it.

"How much power may I use, Ken?"

"Depends on the state of the lake in the morning. If it's dry enough and we can get sufficient adhesion for the wheels, I should try it up to ninety-five per cent. At that I reckon you should have all the acceleration you want to get up to 420 by the sixth mile."

"Provided the salt takes it."

"Provided the salt takes it. That's what worries me. The adhesion can change a couple of points in half an hour, and I don't have to tell you what happens if you lose adhesion when you're accelerating on ninety-five percent power."

"No, old sport, you don't have to tell me at all." Campbell lit himself a cigarette, inhaled deeply, and looked hard at Norris. The memory of Utah was still dogging them. There was no need to repeat what happened when a car lost adhesion approaching 400.

"So you'll leave it to the morning before you make a final decision on the power?" Campbell said at last.

"I think that's the only way," said Norris, and added that as far as he could see the other uncertainties about the car looked as if they would be all right. The response to steering seemed satisfactory after a period when Campbell had been complaining of oversteering, a too-violent reaction to steering-wheel movement at higher speeds. The brakes and the safety parachute were functioning perfectly, and one of the biggest questions, the angle of incidence at which the car should run, seemed to have been settled.

For Norris this had been one of the queries about the car that only prolonged testing at high speeds could really answer. This angle was crucial. From the side the car was shaped like the section of a wing. If the leading edge were raised a fraction too high when the car was traveling at speed, the car would begin to take off. If it were lowered too much, the air pressure on the top of the car would increase and the load on the tires would become excessive. This could make Bluebird uncontrollable and send it right off course. Ideally the aerodynamic load on the car should stay at zero so that the static weight of the car remained on the wheels throughout the speed range. The angle of incidence could be adjusted to allow for this.

"It's difficult to know what further advice to give you about the car," said Norris, closing his file and leaning back in his chair. "I can only tell you it *seems* all right. If the track was right and you felt like giving me half a dozen more really high-speed runs, I might be able to give you more definite answers. But the track's not right. I don't think it ever will be. If you go for the record it's going to be a hair's breadth thing. It has to be your decision."

Later that afternoon Leo Villa gave him much the same advice. "We've checked the old car till there's nothing left to check. It's the worst Goddam course I've ever seen for a car like this, but there you are, Skipper."

But by now Campbell knew that whatever Norris said, the decision had already been taken. Ready or unready, success or suicide, he would have to go now. He made the best of it, talking to his visitors, taking around the drinks, promising Lex Davison that he could drive the car once the record was won, and helping Florence put the champagne in the refrigerator, which was very large and crammed with food. The champagne was the best Australian vintage money could buy.

Perhaps it was the effect of a new audience, perhaps it was his way of relieving the tension, but at dinner he was in better form than he had been for weeks. He joked and laughed nervously, but those like Ken Norris and Leo Villa who understood his mood found it hard to laugh with him. Tonia was another one who seemed more withdrawn than usual. After dinner she sat for a while finishing off a pair of pale blue overalls for Campbell's teddy bear, Whoppit. Then she told him that a letter had just arrived from his daughter Georgina, who was on holiday in Europe.

"She's staying at Como."

"Como, of all places," replied Campbell. "And I suppose you'll tell me next that she's staying at the Villa d'Este."

"Of course."

"My God," said Campbell, putting his hand to his head in mock agony.

"That," said someone, "is what comes of bringing up a daughter to have expensive tastes." And everyone laughed, Campbell as loud as anyone. But it was all unreal, feverish. It needed only the wrong word, the wrong remark, for all this bonhomie to collapse. One was grateful it did not happen.

152

Instead, Campbell stayed on at the homestead after dinner, smoked a pipe, put on his slippers, talked to Tonia, and behaved like the one thing in the world he was not—a comfortably domesticated middle-aged husband. And it was left to the rest of us to go to the 9:00 meeting at the army camp to learn whatever arrangements were being made for the run the next morning.

Here the atmosphere was totally different from the genial coziness that had seemed to protect Campbell up at the homestead. Several more reporters from the Sydney papers had joined Wally Parr, and all of them were out for news, digging away for what one of them kept calling "the real inside story of this man Campbell."

He was a reporter whose mere presence seemed to crystallize disaster out of the air, and the questions he asked caused the first rumors of Campbell's neck trouble to assume a new importance. As we walked to the army camp, he was trying hard to get Norris to talk. Norris did his best to be noncommittal, but his flat, suddenly awkward voice was unable to conceal the anxiety he was feeling.

"He's all right, I tell you. I know him. I've seen all this before. He always gets keyed up before these things, but he's all right. You'll see tomorrow that he's all right."

"But nerves are a terrible thing, Ken. They can make a man freeze up completely. Have you ever seen a man like that, Ken? Have you ever had nerves badly?"

"Look, I tell you the skipper's all right. I've seen him so bad with his back that he had to be lifted into that boat of his. Lifted bodily. Yet six times he went for that record and six times he got it."

It was a dark, cool, dry night. There was a faint wind from the southwest. Rain had fallen again near Alice Springs, but the forecast for the following morning was good, and the cooks in the army camp were already hard at work cutting

153

sandwiches for the hundred or so people expected on the lake at dawn next morning.

There must have been more than sixty people crammed into the big tent the army used as an orderly room for the meeting that night. More than ever now the circus seemed about to start. There was a smell of canvas, of tobacco smoke, of dust, of sweat, of heavy clothing. The public relations officer for one of the cigarette companies was telling one of the specialist engineers in a loud voice, "While you're here you can have all the cigarettes free that you can decently smoke." It was that sort of evening.

The four stewards from the Confederation of Australian Motorsports, who had flown in the previous afternoon, were there, further evidence for anyone who wanted it of how near we must now be to the record bid. They were there to enforce the rules of the Fédération Internationale Automobiliste. Without them no record could be officially recognized, and their presence lent an additional touch of seriousness to the meeting. These stewards were not just four ordinary Australians. They were the international jurisdiction. Here in this tent with its flickering lights and the dust underfoot and the nearest railhead forty miles away, they represented the world. On the following morning they would decide, on behalf of the rest of the globe, whether Campbell's performance entitled him to call himself the fastest man upon it.

I sat near two of them. One, a tall, gray-haired man with a long beard and a kangaroo-skin coat, looked like a younger brother of Father Time. The other, a heavy man with a large mustache, was wearing an army sweater and had a gold filling that half covered one of his front teeth.

They were serious men, and when I asked them about their duties they looked cautious as if guarding some inner truth

154

which they were not overanxious to reveal. The man in the beard explained impressively that the stewards "exercised supreme jurisdiction over the event."

"We," he went on, "can stop it if we feel that the F.I.A. regulations are being broken."

But what were the F.I.A.'s regulations?

He shuffled papers in his hand and I caught sight of one headed "Fédération Internationale Automobiliste." It had a Paris address and was signed by an "M. Schroeder, Gen. Sec." Sensing my interest, he pushed them quickly into the pocket of the kangaroo coat.

"Safety matters," he said. "If spectators were getting too close and we thought this was an undue hazard to themselves or the driver. . . ."

The man with the gold tooth joined in. "We also have to make sure that his documentation is completely in order—that he has his racing permit from the R.A.C. and his driving license, and we issue a track license of our own once we have checked the length of the measured mile and the measured kilometer and gone over the timing devices.

"As well as this," he went on, "we act as replenishment observers, checking that all the activities of the mechanics during the hour allowed between runs are confined to minor things like tires, oil, and small adjustments. There must be no larger repairs to the car, otherwise a driver could go one way and then rebuild his car before driving back."

His gold tooth suddenly twinkled as he laughed, and I asked him what he did for a living. "Oh, this business here is quite honorary. I'm a bit of a car enthusiast in my spare time. I'm a company director."

"Of what?"

"Well, off the record. Campbell would have forty fits if he knew. I'm a funeral director. Biggest in Melbourne."

For some reason the formalities the stewards brought with

155

them that evening were reassuring, confirming that all the anxiety and absurdity of the last few weeks at Lake Eyre was now going to take its place in an ordered, tradition-conscious world—a long-established, slightly dated world of wealthy European aristocrat automobilists, men with obscure titles and heavy overcoats roaring along oil-soaked, long-forgotten race tracks in Darracqs and Sunbeams and Hispano-Suizas in a splendor of dust and goggles and spoked wheels and external brake levers. Lake Eyre was simply the place where the racing car ended.

The seriousness of the stewards was echoed by Cliff Brebner when, as the man in charge of police arrangements for the next morning, he began explaining the rules that would govern all visitors to the lake.

"No vehicle will be allowed across the causeway onto the lake after zero-six-four-five, repeat zero-six-four-five hours tomorrow morning. No apologies will be allowed from any-one arriving after that. Anyone arriving later simply will not get onto the lake."

And Evan Green, as one of the administrators of the run, gave the meeting its final macabre touch. "We mean," he announced, "to have the car rolling by 8:00 A.M. There will be one low-speed run to test the extended track. Subsequent runs will take place at higher speeds. During all these runs the airplane with the doctor aboard will be flying overhead. Should an emergency occur requiring the plane to land, only official police, army, or project vehicles should go near the scene of the emergency. Provided everyone observes this, I think we are fully covered in case anything, repeat *anything*, goes wrong."

But what could go wrong? It was not just the course that seemed the uncertain factor now. No one could tell what would happen the next time Campbell was alone in his cockpit with nothing to do except put his foot down as hard as it would go.

As he went off to bed at 9:30, there was not a man alive who would not have been afraid. What mattered was what he did with his fear, and what his fear did with him.

And there was to be yet another delay. During the night the wind increased, and by dawn it was reported to be blowing directly across the course at ten miles an hour, making any chance of holding Bluebird on its narrow track at 400 clearly impossible. The run was again postponed.

It was as if the lake were waging a war of nerves on Campbell, and the effect of one more postponement after he had keyed himself up to run that morning was perhaps the cruelest thing it had done to him yet.

Tonia was finding it more difficult now to hide her anxiety from him. He was depending on her to an extent she had never known before on a record attempt. When she had been with him on the boat records he had always made a great show of his independence so that she had felt little more than a spectator while the trials were on. Now it was different, and her very honesty made it hard for her to keep up the calm and unconcern he needed so badly from a woman.

She was worried about his neck, too. The effect of the prolonged tension was to make the muscles at the back seize up almost entirely, and for several days the displaced vertebrae had been giving him constant pain. Until now he had not spoken much about it—there had been enough depressing talk. But that Sunday morning the pain was so bad that he had to do something about it.

Campbell has an almost mystical faith in anyone who has treated him successfully in the past, and now he decided that Mr. Charles should make a special trip from Adelaide to treat him.

"He's a wizard," said Campbell, putting his hand behind his neck in the gesture most of us had grown familiar with. "If I can only get him here he'll have me straightened out in no time. He's got a clinic in Adelaide. Charges a flat fee of ten shillings whatever he does for you. He's done more good with his two hands than most doctors with a hospital full of equipment."

So little Mr. Charles, former pharmacist and qualified physiotherapist and osteopath, was flown into Muloorina by Peter Ahrens, who made a special flight to fetch him. For Campbell the pain in his neck was so bad that it seemed to swamp all his other troubles. When the plane landed at dusk with Mr. Charles on board, it was as if the answer to all his troubles had arrived in one man.

Mr. Charles had an air of knowing efficiency common to many of his calling. After a half hour session with Campbell in his room he emerged to announce that yes, the neck had been bad. Three vertebrae had been seriously out of place, resulting in great pain and pressure on the nerve, but now they were back where they belonged and Campbell would have little to worry about.

He smiled shyly as he said this, blinking at us through large spectacles.

"I'll give him another massage just before he goes off to sleep," he said quietly to Tonia. "You'll find that he'll rest well after that. The pain's gone already."

He refused a drink, and said he would have to be flying back to Adelaide at first light. None of us could have guessed, looking at him, quite what repercussions his visit was to have for Campbell and the entire Bluebird project.

CHAPTER THIRTEEN

THE wind that caused such trouble on Sunday disappeared on Monday. Its going was as abrupt as its coming. Just before Monday's dawn the sky became still and full of stars. The first cocks were crowing and the run for which Campbell had waited nine long years was finally on. The first sign of it was when Leo Villa, who never slept, or at least never seemed to sleep, came with his flashlight to wake up his mechanics, who were slumbering along the verandah.

"Go away, you old devil," mumbled a voice, and then one by one the rest of us woke and began struggling into clothes in the dark.

Campbell's greatest privilege that morning was to fly down to the lake just after 7:00 instead of making the dawn exodus with the jeeps, the cars, the yellow Toyota fueling wagons, the ambulances, the breakdown trucks, on their dusty convoy to the lake. Even so, it was too early for his liking. He hates the early morning, and looked tired and depressed as he climbed into the plane along with Tonia, Mason, MacLeonard, Dr. Burke, and a REME major he had promised a lift the previous night.

No one asked about his neck, but he seemed to have developed fresh lines beneath his eyes overnight and had shaved badly. He was holding Tonia's hand very tightly.

159

Conversation was difficult, and the silence in that cramped little plane as it took off and circled up and away to the lake was uncomfortable. The engines roared. Everyone stared ahead, rigidly minding his own business.

"Donald," said a sudden voice from the other side of the cabin, "would you mind counting from one to ten?" It was Dr. Burke in combat suit, horn-rimmed spectacles and dark blue RAAF cap, who was sitting on the far side of the cabin.

"One two three four five six seven eight nine ten," replied Campbell, his lips scarcely moving, his voice already a voice from beyond the tomb.

"Good. *Good.*" Dr. Burke's encouragement was affirmative, contrasting strangely with the apparent passivity of Campbell.

The lake was already coming into view below. There was the line of the shore and the mud with its thin frosting of salt crinkling like scorched paintwork, the thicker salt beyond with its neater pattern of hexagonal cracks, and the pearl, rose, green, silver layers of the lake itself, and the sun rising above the bright rim of the horizon.

"How are you feeling now, Donald?" came the voice of Dr. Burke.

Campbell's reply was inaudible.

"Good, *good*," said Dr. Burke. "Now, Donald, would you mind just fixing this over your face."

From somewhere the doctor had produced a small bag of opaque white plastic. A narrow plastic tube was attached to one end, leading to a small cylinder of carbon dioxide, and two elastic bands were fixed to the other. It fitted across the face like something children wear at Christmas parties.

"That's right, Donald. That's right. The bands around the ears. Good. *Good.* Not too deeply, Donald. Just normally. Perfectly normal breathing, please. Pretend it just isn't there."

The rest of the passengers tried not to notice what was

160

going on, as above the roar of the motors came the sudden hiss of carbon dioxide and Campbell began to inhale. As much of his face as was visible above the mask and the elastic bands was ashen.

"That will do, Donald." The hissing stopped. "Now you have nothing to worry about."

On a record run success depends on a number of apparently minor factors. The effect of speed is to magnify. An ounce of salt on the rim of a wheel grows into a force that shakes a car to pieces at 400 miles an hour. A bump in the track that a saloon car would fail to notice at 40 miles an hour could deliver a car like Bluebird a blow of several tons when traveling at speed.

It is the same with the man who drives her—any weakness, any disequilibrium builds up, distorts, becomes one more source of danger. No one knew this better than Campbell. There was something contradictory in what was being demanded of him. With one part of him he had to forget all fear and commit himself unreservedly to the track, pushing his foot down the full four inches the throttle would travel. It had to be done like an act of faith or an act of love without thought for the consequence.

But with another part of him he had to hold himself in check even while he was risking everything. Never for a moment could he forget the knife-edge he was traveling. The slightest excess on his part, either of power or of steering, the slightest unpremeditated reaction could kill him on a track like this.

There was a certain amount that others could do for him. Leo Villa, for instance. In the two and a half hours the old man had been on the lake before Campbell's plane touched down, he and his assistants had been through the whole routine of double-checking the car for the last time—removing the wheels, testing the brakes and the suspension and the fuel pumps and the brake controls and the compressed air valves and the steering and the throttle.

Norris had his responsibilities as well. He had done his best to estimate the holding power of the salt and to work out the greatest kick it could bear from Bluebird's wheels before the salt disintegrated and left them to spin out of control.

"You've a track length of 13.8 miles," he said to Campbell, "and we've set the engine to give you eighty-five percent power. On that you should be able to take her straight up and still be accelerating as you go through the measured mile at something over 400."

It sounded easy as he spoke, and Campbell nodded and said nothing. It was difficult to know how he was and whether he was up to it or not. He looked calm enough now, but then, with so many more people to watch him than there had been on any of his previous runs, no man as concerned with appearances as he was would have looked any other way. He had a few minutes to wait between talking to Norris and clambering into the cockpit, and it was very still.

Until now everything had been exciting with a lighthearted excitement. Most of the people who had come for the weekend had managed to stay on—Mason and MacLeonard, the millionaire and his beautiful wife, the bony old man from Oodnadatta and his son.

These and many more had made the dawn journey to the lake and seen the sun come up, so close and huge over the horizon that it seemed one more trick of nature the lake put on to scare away its visitors. They had felt the night wind drop as the sun's rays grew stronger, and the two red and yellow Dunlop flags by the stewards' tent drooped in the stillness. They had seen the ambulances arrive, the big army wrecker with the skull and bull's horns still on the radiator,

162

and had watched Villa and his team making the last preparations for the car to run.

But now that Campbell had arrived and was standing alone by the car, the light-heartedness went. The talking stopped. There was a wait while the stewards made certain that Dr. Burke was in the aircraft at the required spot above the course, and at 8:16 the cable from the booster motor was cast off, the stewards clicked their stop watches, and Bluebird roared away with one and only one intention—to go faster than Cobb and faster than Breedlove, to travel faster than any car of any type had traveled on land before.

At the south camp they had the radio receiver picking up Campbell from the car. As they waited for him to appear they heard the breathing, still heavy despite the carbon dioxide, and his voice, thick, slightly slurred by the opening and closing of the valves in the oxygen mask as he repeated the figures from the speedometer with the car accelerating toward the mile. Reception was clear, surprisingly clear, and the figures came between each breath. "Two-ninety . . . 300 at the fourth mile . . .320 . . . 335," the voice counted its way forward.

"She's going through. She's going through. I'm holding her but she's through," said the voice, and then there were no more words. The radio faded and the south camp had to wait, not knowing what had happened. Others were waiting along the track. Tonia in the Morris 1100 near the time-keepers' trailer saw the car streak past the tripods of the timing cameras trailing salt, saw the car seem to hesitate in the very middle of the mile, then sway slightly to one side before sweeping on.

Lex Davison, a little farther on, saw it streak out of the mile, still accelerating.

Norris and Villa inside one of the Valiants were already

163

racing off along the service road to the southern camp to be there when Campbell opened the cockpit.

"You think he had enough power?" Villa asked.

"On this track I couldn't risk him with more," replied Norris.

It had been fast, very fast, but speeds of this level are hard to judge by eye, and no one knew whether he had done it or not.

Not even when the canopy lifted and Campbell sat there shaking his head did anyone know for sure. At first he seemed numbed.

"I'd say 380," he said at last when Villa leaned over to ask him what he thought he had done. "The wheels were going through the surface of the salt from the third mile on. It felt just as if the old car was ploughing its way through slush. Just like slush. Like a great brake holding us back all the time."

Evan Green came across from the control car where the radio had just picked up the official timing from the time-keepers.

"Three eighty-nine, Donald." It was the highest yet. It was five miles an hour short of the record.

He had failed, but he still seemed tantalizingly near to success. The record is the average of the two journeys through the measured mile, and if only he could increase his speed a few miles an hour on the return run he could still beat Cobb.

The lines, the anxiety, were back in Campbell's face, and as he sat there on the edge of the cockpit it was as if the realization of what he had to do was seeping into him a little at a time.

"Cobb made only 378 on one of his runs for the record," said Evan Green.

"How fast would I need to go to make it on this next run?" said Campbell, looking hard at Norris.

"Four twenty-seven," he replied. It was possible if the

164

power was increased. There was another fifteen percent the turbine could give, and fifteen percent should easily be enough to carry the car through that extra twenty miles an hour he needed. But this would be suicide if the track really was collapsing now, if the car had been on the very edge of disaster on its first run, and Campbell had just managed to pull it through.

Once again we were back with the question no one could answer. The question of how much risk a record-breaker should be asked to take or allowed to take.

It was a crucial moment. Campbell was still keyed up enough to have put his foot down, and if Leo Villa or Norris had taken the responsibility of nodding and saying, "Give her maximum power," he would have agreed then and might have just got away with it. He might just have been able to hold the car on its narrow course, just have stopped the wheels spinning at the intersection of the old main track where for four hundred yards the surface of the salt was at its wettest and softest. He might even have scraped the extra twenty miles an hour he needed and become world champion that morning.

Or he might have killed himself.

But Leo Villa and Norris kept quiet. This was not their decision any more. It was up to Campbell.

The turn-around team was hard at work now. The car was already jacked up on its rams, the covers off the wheel fairings, the mechanics in their overalls changing wheels, checking oil, gear-box temperatures, radio, oblivious of the decision Campbell was having to make.

"It's the salt again, Unc," he said suddenly. "That damn salt. I'm digging great furrows in it." He paused, turned away, and for a moment it seemed as if he knew that talking about the salt at this stage was useless. Either he went for the record or he called it off. That was all he had to decide, and just then it looked as though he were going to shut his mind to everything except getting back into the cockpit and calling for the power he needed and putting his foot down.

"How deep d'you think the ruts were, Skipper?" asked Villa.

"I don't know. All I know is that every so often there was a surge forward as if the car was in water, and then it would be held back again when the wheels went in the ruts. Why don't we go and have a quick look? See just how much damage we've done. Have to be quick, mind you, but we *must* see how bad those ruts really are."

It was a mistake, of course. In every way it was a mistake. No one in the middle of risking his neck should pause and try to assess the danger all over again. And it looked bad to have a world contender squandering so many of those bare sixty minutes he possessed for his two runs in inspecting the track.

Nevertheless he went, in the gray, lake-stained Valiant with Ken Norris driving and Leo Villa beside him and Evan Green in the back seat. And when he came to the sixth mile of the course where the car had been under full power and had burned into the salt in two long straight scars that stretched from horizon to horizon, he stopped the car and got out and took his silver lighter to measure the depth of the ruts and said, "For crying out loud, Unc, look at it. Look what the power does to it. We've not a hope in hell."

"We shouldn't have brought him here," said Evan Green to Norris. "He shouldn't have had the sight of this to worry him on top of everything else."

They climbed back into the Valiant and drove onto the center of the measured mile itself. The performance was repeated, with Campbell and Leo Villa probing the salt and standing silent, white-faced, both of them in the middle of that glaring emptiness.

166

By now all the calm, all the resolution that Campbell had been so carefully guarding all morning had gone. He was beginning to talk too much and with him this is always a bad sign.

"Look at it. What a hope we've got. Forget it. Let's all forget the whole damned business." He ground his heel furiously into the salt making a dent an inch deep with water at the bottom. "This course will never get dry. There's a jinx on it. It's this lake, this damn lake. It's out to get me and this morning it nearly succeeded. Look up there." And he pointed to the south end of the course, and everyone could see the way his deep tracks veered right away from the straight blue dye line marking dead center until they were a few feet from the rough, ungraded surface of the rest of the lake. It was only near the end of the measured mile that the tracks got back again to the guide line.

"That's what happened when I nearly lost her. You get a swerve like that and you smash the whole thing."

His left hand was massaging the back of his neck again. "That's what happens, isn't it, Ken? You end up smashing the whole damned thing. I tell you, Ken, this scares me. It scares me stiff."

And it scared the rest of them, too—that was the trouble. It convinced them that if they allowed him to go ahead and push full power through a course in this state they would spend the rest of their lives with his death on their consciences. Nobody spoke on the journey back to the south camp where Bluebird had already been waiting—checked, refueled and ready to drive—for more than twenty minutes.

Everyone was on edge by now and no one, not even Campbell, knew what was to be done. For him the situation was intolerable. He had come to the lake that morning prepared for anything. At the start of that first run he had made himself believe that it could be done. He had shut his mind to the odds against him, to his doubts about himself, to all those nameless fears of something against him that would prevent him getting the record on Lake Eyre.

But now that he had seen the evidence for himself it was hard to avoid the truth. The lake was against him, and however many charms he carried on his key ring, however carefully he avoided green or Fridays or spilling salt, he would end up killing himself if he pushed his luck any farther.

For the people who were waiting, the issue was nothing like so clear. All they knew was that the wind was rising, the salt getting wetter, the minutes ticking past. None of them knew what Campbell knew or had to fear what he feared.

He had been within five miles of the record on one run and now, instead of turning round and going back those few miles an hour faster to beat Cobb, he was sitting on the step of the Valiant, rubbing his neck and showing no sign of moving.

His wife was the only person who really knew what he was up against. She knew that his fear was no ordinary fear. She knew how involved was the battle he was fighting with himself. She knew about his superstition. She understood everything that was at stake for him now, and how the very burden of all this was making his risk so much greater than it looked.

And because she understood, there was nothing she could do, except sit and wait in one of the cars and show him, just by being there, that she was not anxious and that he could do what he had to.

"I don't know what your intentions are, Mr. Campbell, but your hour's nearly up. Unofficially I would say that you have seven minutes left, but I emphasize it's unofficial."

This was one of the stewards, and his formality came as a reminder that the attempt was still on, that something was still expected of him. It produced a sudden effect from Campbell, the sort of desperate, emotional reflex of which he was always capable.

"Ken!" he shouted. "Ken. Let's get it done. Increase the power. I'm taking her back. Quick as we can." Suddenly he was away from the car, running toward Bluebird, and everyone started scurrying after him to get him away while there was still time. His shoes, his helmet, Whoppit the bear, were rushed to the cockpit. The booster motor whined, the timekeepers were informed he was on his way, and he roared off with an extra five percent of power.

It was partly for his own sake that he went. He had to prove that he could still do it. It was partly for the others. He had to show them he had not lost his nerve. It was brave and it was desperate, but it was quite pointless. He made a speed of just over 360 and then hit an exceptionally wet patch of salt and felt Bluebird going out of control. He nearly lost her then and had to ease her down before the mile. And even if he had not, even if he had added the twenty miles an hour he needed to his previous speed, he still would not have got his record.

For the steward had been right to emphasize the unofficial nature of the seven minutes he said Campbell had left. When the time-keepers checked Bluebird's second run through the measured mile, they found he was already eight and a half minutes over the hour. He had been outside it before he even stepped into the cockpit.

CHAPTER FOURTEEN

"THERE'LL be trouble now," said Tonia. "I know all the signs. I've never seen him as patient as he's been here at Lake Eyre. But he's not a patient man, and no one can go on forever taking disappointments like he had this morning."

She spoke with detachment and a certain pride now, as if describing some phenomenon of nature over which she had no control. Around her neck she wore a small golden ram's horn on a long thin chain, which she twisted between her fingers as she talked. "There's a devil in him, you know. It's what drives him on. Usually he keeps it hidden, but whenever he feels cheated of anything it breaks out. He's feeling cheated now. You saw the way he was when the stewards asked him all those questions after the run. That man with the long whiskers and the leather coat asking him why he started a few minutes late and why there had been a delay between the two runs. D'you think that Donald would normally put up with that sort of thing? But you noticed how he got, very quiet, very British. That's always a bad sign with him."

Since the failure of the record bid that morning, the one topic of conversation had been what Campbell would do now, for with this unpredictable, chameleon-like man the

170

next move was always uncertain, and failure seemed to have inspired him with fresh energy.

At first it looked as if he was going to postpone everything until September. He had come back to the homestead, refused lunch, and sat at the dining-room table discussing the chances of reassembling his specialist engineers in two or three months' time when the lake had hardened. "This car of yours is wonderful, Ken. This morning it did far more than any of us had a right to expect. But if we go on we're just going to smash it up. And at this stage of the game that's the one thing I'm not prepared to do, even if it means all the expense and disappointment of waiting until September."

"But have you any certainty that conditions will be any better in September than they are now?" asked Norris wearily.

"Ask old Elliot here. He's the expert on the lake. What's it going to be like here in September, Elliot?"

The old man had been concentrating on his bread and cheese. At Campbell's question he laid down his knife and looked very wise.

"Well, Don, could come good." He munched thoughtfully. "Could go crook on you, too. Hard to tell. All depends when it rains. From now on's the time we hope for it. If we don't have a couple of inches between now and September things'll be looking pretty rough for me'n the sheep."

"What about some other part of the lake then, Elliot? It's a big place. D'you know of anywhere at all now where we could get a stretch of hard salt free of islands?"

"Well, there's Jackboot Bay, fifty miles or so to the west. I flew over it a month or two back and the salt looked hard from the air. It might suit you."

"But what good's that?" said Norris. "We've thought of Jackboot Bay before, but we'd never get Bluebird onto it. There's no road. There's no causeway onto the salt. It would take another month or so to get established there, even if the salt was any good."

"Well, we can't just sit around talking. At least we can go and see. Will you come with me, Elliot, and show me the place you're thinking of?"

Campbell already had his khaki knapsack over his shoulder and was drumming impatiently on the table with his lighter. "We'll take the Aero Commander," he added.

"Sure, Don. Let me finish my tea and I'll come. If I can help you get that record now, I'm game for anything."

Once the plane had taken off, the recriminations started.

One by one the visitors had left. MacLeonard of Ampol had been the first to go. "Sorry I can't stay," he had said as he climbed aboard the company plane, his dispatch case bloated with papers, "but our people have just struck oil in Western Australia. We've been looking for it for fifteen years. Now it seems we might have it at last, and they need me back in Sydney."

The millionaire and his beautiful wife were the next to go. They flew off from Muloorina in a small, sleek, yellow monoplane with two very powerful engines that blew the dust up from the runway into a red cloud that hung in the air some time, signaling their departure.

Florence left before lunch in the charter plane she booked to take her to Adelaide. She left behind the six bottles of Great Western champagne, unconsumed in the refrigerator. "It's good champagne," she shouted. "I'll be back to drink it with you. Make sure you keep it cool, everyone."

All that afternoon there were rumors about the stewards.

"I don't understand what they're up to," said Wally Parr, "but there's something cooking. They won't say anything to the press and they had a long session with Andrew Mustard. They were questioning Norris this morning, too, you know. When the second run was over and they'd had a word

172

with Donald, they asked Ken to stay behind and examined the track with him. They all looked very grim. There's some-one else, too, they seem very interested in."

"Who's that?"

"Campbell's doctor, Burke. He's up at their tent in the army camp now."

I left Parr and walked toward the creek. The water was a greenish yellow and the high soda content made it useless for irrigation. The mud along the banks where the cattle had been was frosted with small white crystals.

A late afternoon wind had begun. Geese and ibises with their large, delicate, fan-shaped wings were flying in to roost, and behind them followed the storm clouds like range upon range of black mountains driven down from the north.

Nearer the homestead the shores of the creek joined the dumping ground for the sheep station, and I was soon pick-ing my way through broken bottles, whisky crates, sheep skeletons, sacks, old boots hidden among the wattle bushes. Near a windowless car crows were pecking at the bodies of two small gray kangaroos. They lay neatly side by side like a freshly murdered married couple.

The birds shuffled as I approached, then flew languidly away, cawing. Then a small boy with fair hair rode up on a bicycle with a pair of rusty rabbit traps dangling from the handlebars. I recognized him as one of Elliot's grandsons.

He took no notice of me, got off the bicycle, and then started burying the two traps in the sand a few inches from the corpses. He worked deftly, frowning slightly as he con-centrated on setting the jaws with a hair trigger and then trickling dust across the platform of each trap and smoothing the sand round them until they were invisible.

"Why do you do that?" I asked.

"For the crows," he said.

"Why?"

173

"Don't know. We just catch 'em, m' cousin and me. Stupid bastards, crows."

It was some time after 5:00 when I returned to the homestead. The Aero Commander was back already, and Campbell was in the sitting room with Ken Norris. His face was slightly flushed and he looked excited.

"Here," he said. "D'you want to hear something to make you laugh, something really funny?" He smiled that forced, small-boy's smile of his. His hair was rumpled. The collar of his blue shirt had got tucked beneath the neck of his darker blue sweater, revealing the nylon cord of the gold St. Christopher medal his father gave him.

"D'you know what they've done—the stewards and our good doctor? They've decided to take exception to the fact that I invited my friend Mr. Charles to come and take a look at my neck. They say it gives them grave doubts about the state of my health and fitness to drive. And they're coming to deliver an ultimatum about it at 6:30 this evening. Funny, isn't it? Really funny. First this morning and now this."

He paced across the room and back. He was wearing his old blue slippers. The leather was slightly scuffed and the backs broken down.

Ken Norris looked tired and worried. There was no further news about his wife, but he had been counting on the record being won that morning so he could fly back to Sydney with MacLeonard.

"I don't understand, Don," he said. "I just don't understand what everyone's up to."

"I do," said Campbell. "All too well I do."

"Take it easy, Don," said Norris. "I know how you feel. After what you went through this morning, it's beyond me how anyone can do this to you. But don't do anything silly.

You've more at stake than anyone. For God's sake, be careful."

"Ken, old scout, I've been careful too long. That's been
my trouble."

"What are you going to do, then?"

"I've asked the press to be present this evening when the
stewards make their announcement. Every word they say is
going to be on the record."

He saw the expression on Norris' face. "Don't look so worried, Ken. It doesn't suit you. The time's come for a show-
down, that's all."

It was an uncomfortable occasion as we waited for the
stewards in the Prices' sitting room. Campbell sat at the
head of the room in the large wooden armchair from the
dining room, his back to the empty fireplace. On his left
were Evan Green and Dick Mason of Ampol, who had decided not to travel back with his boss to Sydney. Wally Parr
was the only journalist there, and Ken Norris was next to
him. We sat in silence.

At 6:30 on the dot a car drew up outside and headlights
glared through the badly cracked frosted glass of Elliot
Price's front door. A car door slammed, and Campbell drew
himself up in his chair and breathed so deeply that the
tendons of his neck showed. He was tense and pale.

The first of the stewards to enter was the bearded orchardist in the kangaroo-skin coat. He was followed by the gold-
toothed Melbourne undertaker and Andrew Mustard.

"Good evening, gentlemen," said Campbell. "And what
can I do for you?"

The undertaker was holding a piece of thin typing paper
headed "Notice from Stewards to Donald Campbell," and I
caught sight of their signatures at the bottom in quavering
blue ink.

"We have something we would like to communicate to you," said the orchardist, tugging at his beard.

"Please be seated, gentlemen," said Campbell. "And just one thing before we start. I would like to remind you that the press are present. Everything we say here tonight is going to be very much on the record and you continue at your peril."

He sat bolt upright, chin drawn in, hands gripping the side of the chair. The two stewards sat and looked equally uncomfortable.

"We would request," said the undertaker, "that we have a private audience."

"Gentlemen, I am not disposed to giving private audiences. I repeat, anything that is said must be said in public." And to complete the formalities Campbell went around the room introducing us all one by one: "Mr. Walter Parr, representing the Australian Associated Press, Mr. Dick Mason of Ampol, and Mr. Andrew Mustard. Whom do you represent, Mr. Mustard?"

"I am here at the request of the stewards," said Mustard, looking understandably puzzled, "and as reserve driver of Bluebird."

"And may I make myself plain. You are relieved of your duties as reserve driver and discharged from my employ, effective immediately."

Before Mustard could reply, the undertaker had stepped forward to deliver his piece. He read from the typewritten paper and invested his words with rich legality like a summons read before a court.

"Notice from Stewards to Mr. Donald Campbell." He cleared his throat. "It has been brought to our notice that on May 26th one or more osteopaths were brought to Muloorina to treat Mr. Donald Campbell for complaints that were not disclosed to our medical officer, Flight Lieutenant

176

Burke, and that may endanger his ability to handle Bluebird at high speeds. We therefore deem it prudent and proper under Rule N.C.R. 122 to insist that Mr. Donald Campbell have a medical examination before being allowed to continue driving."

He finished and sat down heavily on the sofa, wiping his mustache with a large handkerchief. There was silence in the room. Campbell spoke.

"When I was informed that you two gentlemen were coming here to see me this evening, I took the liberty of putting a call through to your general secretary in Melbourne, Mr. Don Thompson. I suggest that you now telephone him straight away for yourselves and read this message over to him. The telephone is here."

This suggestion caught the stewards unprepared. Whatever reception they had been expecting, it had clearly been nothing like this public counterattack.

"Very well then," said the undertaker, and put the call through to Melbourne.

For a minute or so he listened attentively to what the fifteen-hundred-mile distant Mr. Thompson had to say.

"Now just hear me a minute, Mr. Thompson," he said. "I'd like to read over to you Rule 122, just as it is in the book." He repeated the words about the stewards having the power to insist on a medical examination for any contender in a record attempt. "And I'd like to emphasize the last line," he said. " 'No appeal shall lie against this decision of the stewards.' You hear that, Mr. Thompson? If you want to fly over here you damn well can. And may I add that I strongly object to Mr. Donald Campbell coming to you over our heads.

"Now, Mr. Thompson, I'm just not standing for that from any competitor whether his standing is as high as his or not.

"We don't make statements to the press—you ought to know that.

"I cannot comment on that because there are gentlemen of the press here at the moment taking down every word of this conversation."

There was a long pause then. Presumably Mr. Thompson at Melbourne was having his say. The rest of us kept silent, watching the uncomfortable undertaker and wondering what he would do next.

"Mr. Thompson," he said. "I have Ken Archibald, the senior steward, here with me and I'd like him to hear what you are saying. Would you mind repeating those last few words while we share this telephone?"

Unfortunately for the two stewards, a telephone is not an object two grown men can share with decorum, especially when one is exceptionally tall and bearded and the other is portly with a very large mustache. But they did their best. They stood together as if practicing a tango, cheek to cheek with only the earpiece of the telephone between them. First one, then the other, would speak.

"You'd better come over and see for yourself," said the orchardist.

"Mr. Thompson," said the undertaker. "Will you please take a plane and get to South Australia straight away."

"We don't intend to resign our stewardship. That's flat."

"Our position is impossible."

"Our position is untenable."

"You're just not in possession of the facts. This is absolutely necessary. We have expert opinion."

"This order is a request for a medical examination. We're just asking him to be examined."

"But why replace two stewards who are simply trying to do their jobs?"

178

"How do you know, sir? What about the danger to the spectators and the time-keepers?"

"That would be very comforting to their widows."

"If you want to replace us, that's okay by me."

"The name is Geoffrey."

"I cannot speak to you any further without becoming very annoyed and agitated."

The conversation ended, and without another word to us the two of them swept out with deathly dignity.

Campbell ignored the whole incident. "The first thing I would like to clear up, gentlemen, is that I asked a very good friend, a physiotherapist mark you, not a chiropractor, to visit me because of some pain I have been having recently with my neck. The second matter is that I have requested Dunlops for your recall, Mr. Mustard, sir."

"That," replied Mustard, *sotto voce,* face the palest pink above orange whiskers, "will not be necessary. My own direct association with Dunlops terminated some while ago."

"Very well. You will be paid through my lawyers."

"And I take it I am at liberty to withdraw my personnel and equipment from the project?"

"Certainly."

Campbell paused and looked around the silent room. "To-day has seen the conditions the car has had to battle with," he said. "It is a tribute to Ken Norris' design and to British industry that Bluebird achieved what she did. I would also like to pay a tribute to the Commonwealth for all the help the project has had.

"As to the unfortunate references to my fitness, I would like to say that together, Leo, Ken, and I hold more records than any other team in the world, past or present, with the sole exception of my father's. I hold an official license from the FIA. Also civilian air pilot's licenses from England,

179

America, and Australia. All of them involved stringent medical examinations—the last in February 1964."

He stopped. The meeting was over, but Andrew Mustard chose to stay a moment longer.

"This afternoon, sir, I asked you if you were giving up. I would like to ask you the same question again. Are you?"

Campbell glared at him, and when he spoke his voice was thick with anger.

"Despite aspersions by poor unfortunate individuals, we don't give up. Good night."

A dazed silence followed Mustard's departure. It took time for the full implication of these last few minutes to sink in. Then one by one we realized that we had probably been listening to the end of the Bluebird project. The fuse was lit now. It would take only a little time for the explosion. Within a few hours it would be front-page news in Sydney and Adelaide—the row with the stewards, the break with Mustard, the doubts cast on Campbell's fitness to drive.

In one disastrous day Campbell would have lost nearly everything he possessed: his track, his official authority to get a record; and he would be at the center of a full-scale controversy that would split the camp wide open and have to be conducted in public. No one, not even he, could hope to survive it.

He must have realized this, too. Just as we were about to leave he spoke to Parr, and for the first time that evening there was a note of caution in his voice.

"Wally, old boy. Just one thing before you go." He groped uncertainly for the right phrase. "Perhaps—if you don't mind —it might be best for the project if we treated all this as off the record."

Parr paused a moment as he was putting his notebook away and there was an uncomfortable silence. It was an unforgivable request to make of any reporter. When he answered he spoke very slowly.

"Very well, Donald. Very well. Although I feel as if I had just been used as a club to beat a lot of people over the head with."

If Bluebird was to survive now, someone had to act as mediator, and it was Norris, sane, worried Ken Norris, who took charge. The first person he enlisted was Evan Green. "Evan," he said, "we must stop this going any further. Enough damage has been done already. If we want to keep the project together we've got to act and act fast.

"First priority is to look after Don, and you're the man to do it. He trusts you and will do what you say. Keep him away from the press and away from the stewards. Explain what's happened to Tonia. He needs sleep desperately. I know him when he's like this. I saw it coming and should have done something about it earlier. It was the strain of this morning's run with the disappointment and frustration on top of everything else. It all boiled up. It's his way of letting off steam. Just get him to bed now and he'll be right as rain tomorrow."

"I'll do my best," said Green. "But where are you going? What's your next move?"

Norris paused at the verandah door and grinned. "I'm going to see Andrew Mustard first and then those stewards. It's in nobody's interests to bust everything up at this stage. I'll get Don to withdraw his dismissal of old Andrew. Then I'm going to calm the stewards down if I can."

"I wish you luck," said Green.

"I'll need it. Just look after Don. He's been pushed a bit too far today."

One of the gray Valiants was standing outside the homestead. Norris got in and started the engine.

"I'll let you know how I get on," he shouted.

As he drove off into the darkness in the direction of the army camp Parr said mournfully, "It was a great story."

"It was," I replied. "Why did you kill it? You didn't have to. I can't think of many reporters who would have acted as nobly as you did."

"It wasn't being noble," he said. "It was sentimentality. Sheer sentimentality. I must be getting old. You see, I like the man. At times there's a wonderful air of innocence about him. And I don't want to see him destroy himself, though he seemed hell-bent on it this evening."

"What will happen if the story does get out?"

"It'll be the last of Campbell—at Lake Eyre, at any rate. It will be the biggest row of his career. There will be an investigation, and whatever the rights and wrongs of the case, he can't possibly afford that sort of thing now. He'll lose his specialist engineers, and the government will probably pull out."

"But *will* it happen, do you think?" I said.

"Probably. I'm not the only press man here now, you know. Peter Michelmore's covering it for the *Adelaide Advertiser,* and his stuff's being syndicated to London. He's only got to persuade Mustard or one of the stewards to talk and there's the whole story ready made. I expect things have gone too far to be patched up now."

Peter Michelmore was tall and tough and charming. More important, he was a free-lance reporter, paid by results. When he called at the homestead within an hour of Campbell's meeting, he knew what he wanted.

Evan Green tried coping with him on the lines Norris

suggested, but it was difficult. He stood awkwardly in the doorway of the homestead as if guarding everything that lay beyond, and Michelmore, fair-haired, decisive with note-book and neatly tailored gabardine golf jacket, had to ask his questions from outside.

"Evan, there's a lot of talk around the camp about a break between Donald and the stewards and Andrew Mustard. I'd like to know how much truth there is in it."

"No comment at this stage, Peter. Sorry."

"Very well then. I'm formally asking you for an interview with Campbell."

"Sorry. That'll have to wait until tomorrow. Don's very tired after the strain of this morning's run and is in bed asleep."

"That makes it very hard for me if I'm to get the story straight. Is there nothing at all you can tell me?"

Green shifted his weight from one foot to the other. "Nothing at all. Donald's very tired and I've no intention of disturbing him tonight."

So the evening ended and the future of the Bluebird project was still in the balance. Campbell slept peacefully. The stars were very bright and there was a cold wind from the north.

Norris' gray Valiant was parked up at the army camp until nearly midnight. Michelmore was busy, too, and it was very late before he had seen all the people he needed, typed his story, and telephoned it over for the morning editions. And in the army tent someone got drunk and threw a canful of Southwark Bitter into the sad Irish face of Dr. Burke. But for the firmness and tact of Superintendent Brebner, there might have been quite a fight.

CHAPTER FIFTEEN

"WELL?" said Evan Green.

"Keep your fingers crossed," Norris said.

"Did you see the stewards?"

"Yes. And Andrew Mustard. He's coming at 9:00 for a meeting with Donald."

"Are we going to get away with it?"

"We might. No one wants direct responsibility for wrecking the project, and there are a lot of second thoughts about what was said and done last night. Let's hope a good night's sleep has done its work."

"What about the press?"

"Some of the story got out, but it's not as bad as it might have been. The Adelaide headlines this morning are 'Rumors of Split in Campbell Camp.' If that's the lot, we can survive."

"What about your wife? Any news?"

"Nothing. I must get home soon. At the moment I'm feeling a bit too responsible for everyone."

It was 8:00 the following morning, and the appearance of the two men on the verandah of the homestead was the first sign of life in the camp. The day seemed reluctant to begin. The crows were cawing from the cattle pens and the sun had risen coldly in the west. Now that the record bid had lost its way, Muloorina had lapsed back to its normal tempo with the wind pump clanking by the creek, the geese nesting

184

among the reeds, the dogs scavenging behind the slaughter house.

"We'd better get some breakfast," said Green.

"I've had mine," replied Norris.

Somehow the news that Andrew Mustard was coming got around the camp, and by 9:00 everyone was outside the homestead to watch him arrive. It was odd. Muloorina had seen nothing like it before, with these small, silent knots of people standing waiting for something to happen: the cameramen in one group, the specialist engineers in another, the mechanics and drivers and military police in yet another. From the homestead they looked ominous, like people waiting for a great man to die or a government to fall.

They heard the clock on the Prices' mantelpiece strike 9:00—a measured, solemn sound—and as it finished the big blue Humber drove up with Mustard at the wheel.

Still no one spoke. No one said "Good morning, Andrew." They just watched as he got out of the car and strode, beard in air, through the screen door with its notice, "Do *Not* Slam." It slammed behind him.

Norris and Evan Green followed him into the sitting room where Campbell had been waiting for some time. There was no sign of the stewards.

Outside the people stayed on. The day became warmer. The crows fell silent. Some of the watchers wandered off for a beer. At 10:30 one of Elliot's grandsons came out of the homestead and walked toward the shearing shed.

"What are they doing in there?" someone asked him.

"Talking."

"Still?"

The boy nodded.

"What's that you've got inside your shirt?" one of the cameramen asked.

"Nothing."

"But I saw something moving."

The boy scuffed in the dust and carefully regarded his shoes.

"It's me dragon. I shouldn't get too near. He'll bite you."

"Can't we see it?" asked the cameraman politely.

The boy examined his shoes a while longer. "All right. I'll put him on the log by the gas pump. He likes it there. But watch out. He'll kill anyone he doesn't know."

Quite a crowd had collected around the boy now, and they followed him over to the log. He reached inside his shirt, and after fumbling a moment brought out a fat brown lizard fourteen inches long with a body as thick as a man's wrist. It looked prehistoric. Its scales shone. When it blinked in the strong sunlight a milk-white eyelid swiveled across a beady black eye.

"He knows me," said the boy, tickling scaly head with grimy forefinger. The animal yawned obligingly, revealing a mouth like a miniature man-trap lined with hard red flesh. "Dragons is real dangerous," he said.

The lizard stayed motionless on its log, and the cameraman decided to film it for want of anything better. They took a lot of trouble, but the small boy remained unimpressed.

It was 11:00 before there was any further sign of life from the homestead. Evan Green came out, a sheet of paper in hand, a look of troubled sincerity on his face.

"The dispute, gentlemen, has been settled." Campbell's way of speaking was contagious. "The next high-speed run will take place on Thursday. After yesterday's run there are four ruts eight miles long to be filled in with salt, then the course will be left to harden. This will take a minimum of three days. Frankly, gentlemen, we are on a knife edge now. Bluebird was designed for—"

"Excuse me, Evan," said Michelmore, butting in suddenly.

186

"What about the trouble between Campbell and Andrew Mustard? Is Mustard still working for him or not?"

"His position is what it always has been."

"Good. And the stewards. Has that been cleared up, too?"

"Off the record, Peter, I think I can put you in the picture. You will appreciate—"

"I appreciate that I am here to report a story for a newspaper. Too much has been said off the record already. All I want to know is what I can print."

Green looked sad.

"Very well, Peter. All I can say is that we anticipate no major problems over the stewards either."

The terms of the armistice Ken Norris worked out between Campbell, Mustard, and the stewards remained obscure. Mustard had assured Campbell that he had had nothing to do with the stewards' action and returned to his old job. The stewards were not replaced. They remained in the chilly dignity of self-imposed exile up at the army camp and Parr said that when Campbell was ready for his next bid a new doctor would be brought in to examine him. Once this was done there could be no further objections. The crisis, it seemed, was over.

But Campbell seemed despondent about his chances. At dinner that Tuesday he ate little, said little. Dick Mason of Ampol was sitting on his left and did most of the talking. He is a kindly, ingenious man, and he was doing his best to be helpful, but everything he suggested seemed to add to the gloom.

"In Hong Kong our company has the agency for some stuff called Kompak. It's a chemical they spray on to stabilize the surface of dirt roads. I don't see why it shouldn't work on salt. We could always give it a try. Perhaps I'll have some flown up."

Campbell said nothing and pushed away his plate with most of his steak uneaten.

"And have you thought of some sort of matting? If you could get enough of it and lay it along the course that might do the trick. But there'd be the difficulty of fastening it down, I suppose.

"Or how's about the Nullabor Plain," he said. "It looks pretty flat when you go across it on the train from Adelaide to Perth. There's seven hundred miles of it. You ought to be able to find just fifteen that would take Bluebird."

"Dick," said Campbell. "I'm afraid this is all a bit late in the day for us. From now on it's Lake Eyre or nothing."

Thursday's run took place according to plan. Campbell had been examined by a regular Air Force doctor and found perfectly fit and the stewards raised no objections after this. But it was hopeless from the start. A six-mile-an-hour wind was blowing across the track at 8:00 A.M. It increased as the morning went on, and when Campbell took Bluebird up to 300 miles an hour at 9:30, he reported that it was almost impossible to keep her straight.

It seemed as if all the efforts and anxieties of the last few days to keep the project going had been wasted after all. Campbell had survived so much that he deserved something better. But the life had gone out of everything, and even the car looked tired. When the run was over, he went off on his own without talking to a soul.

The sun was hot but the wind was gusting across the lake, flapping the canvas sides of the hangar, blowing Campbell's hair. He stood with his hands in his pockets, his back to us all, staring away to an empty horizon. I remembered what he told me not long after I arrived at Lake Eyre when he had just finished showing me the car and the organization.

188

"You know why I do all this?" he had asked. "Conceit—no other reason when you boil it down. The conceit of believing that this is something I can do better than anyone else in the world. I suppose it's the same with most artists or politicians. Everyone likes to think that they're unique. This is my way of proving it."

And as he stood there by the hangar so completely cut off from the rest of us, I realized that he would keep going—that whatever the odds, he would never give in. This was not merely because he was brave. Brave men will surrender when courage becomes useless. It was his inability ever to accept the fact that he was commonplace like the rest of us. And the more he lost heart, the stronger would be his resolve. For despair is commonplace, and only success would ever convince him that he was still unique.

After that Thursday, time slowed down. It was Campbell against the rest of us now.

"It's impossible," said Parr. "He's punch-drunk. He can't get the record and he can't give up. It's absurd. What hope's he got now?"

"None at all, I should think. But you're dealing with an unusual man here. He doesn't need hope. He just waits. He's done it before with the boat."

"But the boat was different. It didn't have all this great organization. If he wants to wait much longer, he'll soon be here on his own. Brebner's men have itchy feet. So have the track staff. The specialist engineers are getting orders from their firms in England to go home, and Norris is already staying on borrowed time. It can't last much longer."

But it did. The attempt dragged on through Friday and Saturday, and there was still no hope of a record and no sign of giving up.

Leo Villa stuck by Campbell, of course, and Norris carried on loyally with his graphs and his mathematics. But for the rest of us the Bluebird project died that week. All that remained was one man with an obsession. It was as sad and as futile as that.

Tonia had the worst of it. For most of us the only real problem was how soon we could get away. For her it was how her husband could be saved without destroying everything he lived for.

"I've never known Donald like this before," she said. "He's lost heart but he won't give up, and he's getting more and more superstitious. His father's very much in his thoughts now."

"How?"

"It's complicated and I don't entirely understand it myself, but you know Donald's always believed that he was simply continuing where his father left off."

I nodded.

"That's always been desperately important to him. You've seen his father's little Bluebird medal in the car, and you know how he's kept the name Bluebird going. I don't think many sons would have done that, but for Donald it was all part of the mystique.

"Now I've told you this is complicated. In his time he's had some fantastic escapes, and he really believes his father has helped him through. Once in the boat when he lost control he says he knew for sure he was going to die. Then at the last moment some outside force took over and saved him.

"It's all right for people who've never taken a risk in their lives to be skeptical about these things. But Donald believed that by carrying on where his father left off he had some special protection. His father was still there to help him—a sort of guardian angel."

She paused, and her voice was quieter as she went on.

"That's what he used to believe. Now he's not sure. So much has gone wrong. He feels that whatever helped him before has gone."

It was not until Sunday, June 7th, that Campbell was able to run again. The wind kept blowing, and the long ruts in the track refused to disappear, although they had been filled with loose salt and smoothed countless times with the drags.

The previous afternoon he and Norris had met at the lake to decide what was to be done. Campbell knew that Norris would be flying back to England within forty-eight hours and that the specialist engineers would be following him. But that had not been mentioned. They had taken their time examining the track together—Campbell in his blue Ampol jacket, Norris in an ink-stained gabardine wind-breaker buttoned to the neck—and they had not said much, even when they kicked the loose salt crystals packed into the ruts and saw the water still lying on the surface at the intersection with the old main course.

They had driven back to the base camp where Leo Villa was working on the car.

"Tomorrow then, Ken," Campbell had said. "Better make it an early start. Seven-thirty all right with you, Unc?"

The old man had nodded.

"And Ken. It'll have to be one hundred percent power on the turbine. This may be our last chance."

"I can't advise it, Don. I must warn you what you're going to be up against on that track."

"Ken, let's not be silly. We all know what we're up against. But I've got to go and it's not your responsibility any longer. You and Leo have both done your job a hundred times over. Now it's my turn."

Nothing was said to the rest of us about Bluebird running at full power for the first time at Lake Eyre. Gloomily we drove to the lake before light the next morning.

"Another run. Another damned waste of time," muttered one of the cameramen as we jolted our way through the dark in our Land Rovers. "Christ, it's cold. I never knew Australia could be as cold as this."

Half a mile ahead we could see the bobbing tail-lights of the truck in front. Dust swirled in the long yellow tunnels of our headlights. And as we drew near the lake we saw the first sign of dawn, a thin slice of gray cut into the blackness of the west.

The wind still blew as Campbell waited by the car, blue sneakers in his hand, and the slow rigmarole of the start-up began.

"Is this going to be it, then, Donald?" asked Parr.

"Perhaps, Wally. Let's just see."

"Everything all right with the stewards now?"

"Fine. . . ."

It was nearly 8:00 before the wind dropped a little, and Campbell nodded to Leo Villa. He winked at Ken Norris just before the canopy closed. No one spoke as the car roared away. It was a routine now.

Nevertheless, this was a full-scale record bid. Time-keepers and stewards were in their places. Movie cameras were lined up for the start, and long-lensed cameras were already sited on tripods by the measured mile as Bluebird thundered past.

But there was only one run. At the end of it Campbell sat in the cockpit, helmet off, saying nothing. It was not until Norris appeared that he spoke.

"Ken, something happened then that I just don't understand. You're sure you did set the turbine at a hundred percent power?"

"Of course, Don."

"You weren't trying to save my life by keeping the power down, or anything silly like that?"

"No, of course not, Don. What d'you mean?"

"Then it's the end. You can tell the stewards to go home. My foot was down as far on the throttle as it would go. *Yet she was only indicating sixty percent power and wouldn't go higher than 360.* There's a jinx on this lake, Ken. There's something here that none of us understands."

That afternoon Superintendent Brebner of the South Australian Police made a formal visit to Campbell at the homestead. It was a visit he had expected to make sooner or later, but he had not been looking forward to it.

He found Campbell in the dining room, writing letters on the big table. He looked tired and rather ill, with dark patches under the eyes. But he was cheerful enough, rather as patients can be after a serious operation.

"Ah, Cliff," said Campbell. "I was half expecting you. I think I know what you're going to say."

"Well, we can't go on like this, can we, Don? After this morning you're obviously not going to get anywhere with your present track, and I don't think my boys can take much more of this waiting around. It's nearly two months now."

"I know, Cliff, and I'm very grateful. What do you suggest?"

"In my opinion you should postpone now. And quickly, while you've still got the car and everyone's good will. If you hang on much longer I think you'll have real trouble. Leave straight away, then you can come back in a couple of months and your track will have hardened if you're lucky. Take my advice. Let the air clear and the salt harden."

"Okay, Cliff," said Campbell. "You're probably right. Can I let you have a decision this evening?"

Campbell was not really as calm as he seemed, and when Brebner had gone he left the homestead in search of Norris. He found him in his trailer. Books and clothes were piled on the bed, an open suitcase beside them.

"You're off now, then, Ken."

"Sorry, Don. I must get back. The doctors say in a day or two. I should get there just in time."

"Don't apologize to me, old boy. I'm the one who should apologize, keeping you here so long. I'll fly you down to Adelaide first thing tomorrow morning. You'll be in time for the midday plane to Sydney."

With all the mess and muddle of packing the trailer appeared even smaller than usual. It seemed impossible that three men could have lived in it for so long. There were two empty sherry bottles in the sink. The film projector was on the floor. There was a smell of eggs and bacon and male clothing. Campbell sat on one of the unmade beds and lit his pipe.

"Ken," he said, "I know it's all over." Norris stood awkwardly at the end of the trailer. He nodded but said nothing.

"But something happened today, Ken. Something I don't understand. And I'm not leaving here until I find out what it was."

Norris pushed the suitcase off the bed then, and sat down. Campbell took the pipe from his mouth and leaned forward, elbows on knees, staring intently at him.

"You realize, Ken, that I should have been killed today? The wheels got caught in the ruts when I had my foot hard down at full power. By everything we've been led to expect, that car should have gone right out of control. But it didn't. It should have but it didn't. Something was keeping the power down."

He sat a moment longer. From outside came the noise of

Elliot Price's grandchildren playing around the back of the homestead. A dog barked. Campbell puffed at his pipe.

"I'm not leaving Lake Eyre until I've found out what it was. Whatever kept the power down this morning saved my life."

The answer came sooner than anyone expected. That same afternoon Leo Villa and Carl Noble, checking over Bluebird's controls after the run, found a minute leak in the throttle valve. It was so small that it had not shown up before. A little of the hydraulic fluid had leaked away, so that when Campbell put his foot on the accelerator, slightly reduced pressure was transmitted to the engine throttle valve.

Tonia was with Campbell in the sitting room when Norris came in with the news. Campbell shook his head. "It's all very, very odd. Don't you think so, darling?" he said to Tonia.

"Everything's odd here," she said. "If it saved your life that's good enough for me."

"But this is incredible," said Campbell. "At the one moment when I'm for the high jump one tiny valve decides to leak. You're a rational fellow, Ken. Explain that to me."

"It could have happened any time, Don. You were just lucky."

"Lucky be damned. You'll be telling me it was a coincidence next."

He poured some brandy into a large glass, topped it up with soda and passed it to his wife. For the first time in weeks his face showed hope and excitement.

But Norris did not seem so optimistic. "If you'll excuse me, Don, I've still got some packing. I'll see you later." He paused at the door. "It's still all right about Adelaide tomorrow morning?"

Campbell nodded. "Eight-thirty sharp."

When Norris had gone, Campbell turned to his wife and took her hand. "Darling," he said. "You realize what this means? This isn't a coincidence, it's all part of a pattern. And nothing's as bad as I thought. Now I know it's going to be all right."

Campbell called on Brebner that evening up at the army camp. The superintendent had been expecting this to be a tense occasion, but Campbell seemed quite cheerful. He was wearing his old red and white neck-scarf and some color was back in his face.

"Okay, Cliff," he said, smiling and opening his hands as if to show that he had nothing left to offer. "You're right. Absolutely right. We're going to postpone."

It was stuffy in the tent with the smell of canvas and dust and cigarette smoke. Brebner was sitting on his camp bed. The double line of his medal ribbons caught the light from the sixty-watt bulb in the center of the tent. It was he who looked tired now, not Campbell.

"Are you sure this is really what you want, Don? I don't want you to feel I'm pushing you into it."

"No, Cliff, thanks. It's my decision. We'll leave the car here and all the equipment. Leo and the boys can do with a break. So can I. But everything stays where it is and we come back just as soon as we get word that the lake's ready."

"You really will be coming back, then?" Brebner asked slowly.

Campbell seemed puzzled by the question. "We came here for a record, Cliff. So far we've failed to get it."

Campbell announced his decision to the rest of the camp later that night at a meeting in the shearers' quarters, and the exodus from Muloorina started next morning as soon as it was light.

It was a hot, airless day. A pair of eagles was circling above the homestead and an early heat haze made the salt bushes near the army camp seem to dance in the sun's glare. But the circus was folding—noisily, anxiously, with men sweating and shouting to each other in the heat as they roped bags to roof-racks and checked gas and water for the long drive south.

One by one the cars roared off down the track to Marree, past the whitened piles of camel bones, past the deserted tents, across the creek by the gum trees where Elliot Price had marked out his grave.

At 8:30 the Aero Commander took off for Adelaide with Ken Norris and some of the engineers aboard. And by afternoon the only evidence the last two months had left behind was the row of empty trailers beyond the shearers' quarters and a hillock of tin cans, not yet rusted, behind the homestead.

The two eagles were still in the sky when Elliot Price came out on the verandah, yawning from his after-dinner nap. He saw his son-in-law by the barn.

"Well, boy, they've gone," he shouted. "Now we can get down to some work."

He put his thumbs behind his suspenders and gazed at the empty wilderness he owned.

CHAPTER SIXTEEN

FIVE weeks later Campbell and Tonia were sitting in the Hong Kong Restaurant in Melbourne listening to the proprietor, Mr. Philip Liu, muttering ancient Chinese curses against the terrible weather of Victoria. It was after 9:00, but so far only seven other people had arrived. Outside in the rain green streetcars were rattling past. Inside in the warm, Mr. Liu's hi-fi system was playing selections from the incidental operatic music of Donizetti.

Campbell had started the meal with shark's-fin soup and leaned forward to take a second helping, ladling the long, tapioca-like shreds of shark meat from the blue and white bowl before him.

"More for you, darling?"

Tonia shook her head and sat looking out at the lights of the hotel across the road. She was wearing a black and white silk dress that clung to her figure and showed off the warm tan on her face and arms. Campbell had had a good haircut. His face was fuller and the grayness had gone. He wore a single-breasted dark blue suit with cloth-covered buttons and cuffed sleeves, and had recovered the indefinable patina of the international celebrity.

"Nine and a half hours behind Melbourne time," he said. "That makes it 11:00 in England now. If we put the call through in a half hour we'll catch him just before he goes to lunch."

"He'll be surprised to hear you," said Tonia. "Are you sure he'll be able to come out straight away?"

"He'll come. Now that the baby's arrived and doing well, nothing will keep old Ken away."

"I hope you're right. We're certainly going to need him."

She tried to sound enthusiastic, but until tonight she had been quietly hoping that something would happen—she hardly knew what—to keep her husband from Lake Eyre for good.

There had been times during the past month when Campbell's obsession with the lake had seemed to be weakening. Days would go by without his mentioning it. They had traveled together to Sydney for a short holiday, then on to Brisbane, and as her husband picked up his old energy and started enjoying life again, Lake Eyre seemed a long way away. At times he had talked of producing films, or opening some new business. But he had always added, "After the record of course, darling," and she had known better than to argue.

Before the soup was finished, Mr. Liu began piling the table with dishes for the next course—fried rice, boiled rice, chicken and mixed vegetables, prawns Chinese style, bamboo shoots, and mushrooms. Campbell helped himself to a few of his favorite prawns. Then he hesitated and looked uncertainly at her. "This telephone call to Ken. Are you sure you want me to make it?"

"What do you mean?" she said. "If Leo tells you the salt is harder, now's the time for Ken to come, isn't it?"

"No, that's not what I mean. If we're going to back out of this, now's our very last chance. Once Ken and the engineers are on their way there's no going back. Are you sure you want me to go on with it?"

He had never asked her this question before, and she was touched by his concern.

"Yes, I'm sure," she said softly. "Are you?"

"Absolutely. I can't explain it, but I've never been more certain of anything in my life. It's like having a voice inside me telling me I've got to go on."

He began eating. "I can't forget what happened on that last run with the throttle valve," he said. "There's a definite pattern to these things. Believe you me, these things just don't happen by chance, sweetie. There's someone up there keeping a very good eye on yours truly."

"That's all right then," she said.

"But I'm worried about you," he said. "It's no place for you at the lake. You've had more than enough of it already. Are you sure you wouldn't like to stay in Adelaide with Florence?"

"What, with all those temptations for a man at Lake Eyre? I'm coming to keep an eye on you."

As she spoke the door of the restaurant opened and four people came in, shaking the rain from their plastic raincoats. Mr. Liu, beaming now, went forward to meet them, and the record on the hi-fi changed from Donizetti to Offenbach.

"Fine," said Campbell. "That's settled then. Eat up, the prawns are marvelous. In twenty minutes we must be back in the hotel to put the call through to England."

Nothing had changed. There was no reason why it should have, but all the way up to Muloorina on that Thursday afternoon Campbell wondered whether this time it was going to be different. Then he banked the Aero Commander low over the lake and saw the deceptive brown and gold of

200

the salt from five hundred feet and knew that he was back where he had left off.

True, some of the people had changed. He had seen to that. There were two new stewards. He had them with him now in the airplane: Alec Hawkins, an official of the Melbourne Light Car Club, and Dr. Lloyd Buley, deputy chief medical officer of the Department of Civil Aviation. Campbell had taken to them both from the moment they first met in Melbourne, and, unlike their predecessors, they did not seem to feel that their official duties compelled them to keep their distance from Campbell.

Buley, a former RAAF pilot, had lost both legs during the war, but still drove his blue Porsche through the streets of Melbourne and acted as chief medical officer to the Confederation of Australian Motor Sports. A trip to Lake Eyre seemed exactly the sort of outing he enjoyed.

Andrew Mustard was still in charge of Bluebird's tires and wheels. All his former responsibilities for the track and the project as a whole had been split between Evan Green and Campbell's genial friend Graham Ferrett, manager of Yorke Motors in Adelaide. And the postponement had inevitably caused casualties among several of Bluebird's key personnel.

Norris, now the proud father of a four-week-old son called Louis-John, was back, and had brought with him George Hammond of Bristol Siddeley and Ron Willies of Girling. But the Owen organization had not allowed Scrimshire or Noble to return. Reaks, the expert on Bluebird's instruments, was missing, too.

The truth was that the odds against Campbell winning his record now seemed even bleaker than when he called off the attempt at the beginning of June, and the sight of the lake suddenly revived all his own worst doubts. In those last few minutes before bringing in the Aero Commander to land at Muloorina, he went through them again one by one. There was the salt. Would it really be any harder? And money. How much longer could he keep up the expense of the attempt on his own?

As he circled Muloorina there seemed to be no sign of life. The trailers were still there beyond the homestead. The tents of the army camp were exactly as he remembered them. There was the big corrugated iron shed with "Muloorina" painted in black across the roof, and to the right lay the dull red ribbon of the runway.

He looked back at Tonia, then put the plane down hard, keeping the stick pulled into his stomach and the nose up until the last possible moment. Only when the two rear wheels touched the runway and the end of the strip came racing toward him did he ease the nose forward and feel the plane whirring to a halt. He switched off the motors.

"So you're back after all, Donald," shouted someone from outside. "Some of us had our doubts we'd be seeing you again, but we kept your bed aired just in case."

Campbell opened the side window of the cockpit, and saw Elliot Price standing beside his gleaming black car at the edge of the airstrip. He had the same suspenders, the same collapsed gray trilby, the same cautious old sheep-farmer's smile.

"Don't worry about the bed," shouted Campbell. "Have you managed to do anything to the lake?"

"That's all right, Don," said Elliot, nodding sagely. "You'll be surprised what's happened to it while you've been away."

"How soon d'you think, Unc?"

"Well, Skipper, the car's ready. The time-keepers got up here yesterday. Now the driver's arrived we've nothing else to wait for."

Leo Villa grinned and looked at Campbell over the top

202

of his spectacles. For the past five days he and his two assistants, Maurie Parfitt and Brian Coppock, had been back at Muloorina working on Bluebird. More than ever he felt responsible for Campbell, and would have given anything to have had the record bid take place somewhere else. He did not trust Lake Eyre. He never had from the start. But he knew he must keep these doubts to himself now. Nothing could be allowed to shake Campbell's new mood of optimism.

"But what about the lake, Unc?" asked Campbell. "Has the track really improved? What about those damned ruts?"

The note of appeal in his voice was familiar to Villa, for over the years he had heard it many times before. He could remember occasions when young Donald had wanted something forbidden by his father. He had always turned to Leo then, and the old man had learned with experience exactly how to reply—guardedly, conspiratorially, without giving the boy all he wanted, but without refusing him entirely.

"You mustn't go expecting too much, Skipper," he said now. "It's still a lousy track. But it's better, just a shade better, than it was."

"Too late for us to go and have a quick look at it before dark, I suppose?" said Campbell.

"Now take it easy, Donald. There's all tomorrow."

"But I want a run tomorrow. I tell you, Unc, I don't intend to stay in this place a single minute longer than I have to."

But it took longer, much longer, than Campbell had expected. Next morning, he flew to the lake with Villa and Norris and Evan Green and cheerful Ferrett. They visited the car where it had been waiting for them, jacked up inside the hangar. Then they drove up to look at the track.

Everyone was wary now of making any rash pronouncement. They stopped at the measured mile, and saw for themselves that the crust of salt seemed fractionally harder than it had been a month before. Then they waited for Campbell to speak. His was the verdict that counted.

In the distance the big red marker at the start of the mile was flapping in the wind. The sun was bright, glaring, like a great white arc light that allowed no shadows, no privacy, and as Campbell strolled across his track, hands in pockets, occasionally kicking the salt with his heel, he was like a condemned man choosing the site of his own execution.

"It's still pretty soft," he shouted. "Not quite what I was hoping for."

No one replied and his voice sounded small and lost in the great emptiness of the lake.

"But the ruts have hardened over. That's something."

He walked on, then stopped, took out a handkerchief, and held it fluttering in the breeze.

"What about this wind, Unc?" he shouted. "The wind— has it let up at all?"

"No. Seems to be keeping on all the time," Villa shouted back.

The rest of the group saw Campbell nod to himself then, and begin to walk back slowly toward the car. As he reached it he put his hand on Villa's shoulder and they heard him say, "Ah well, Unc. Here we go again."

For the rest of that day until the sun was almost down the team stood by with Bluebird fueled and the starter truck in place and the time-keepers ready by the measured mile, waiting for the wind to drop. It never did. Nor the day after. Nor the day after that. Lake Eyre was under siege. It would not give in easily.

For the small group of people waiting round that stationary blue car, time began to lose all meaning. The lake seemed to be their one environment. It was hard to remember a time when they had not been there, harder still to imagine a time when they would ever get away.

And all day the cold, steady wind blew, and they knew that they would have to outwit the wind but that patience was their only weapon. And because they accepted this, these days of dawn-to-dusk standby were never hopeless like the delays and endless disappointments of May had been.

Campbell waited calmly now, like a man who knew his chance would come. His party was a better unit for survival than it had been. Every member knew what to expect. The old battles within the project were burned out, and instead of being disappointed with each failure his people now were in a mood to be grateful for the smallest success.

This was just as well, for on Sunday night, after three days of waiting, the wind was blowing as strong as ever. When Campbell listened to the evening weather forecast on the radio he learned that there was no chance of a let-up. Worse still, rain was said to be on the way again.

"What the hell do we do now, Skipper?" asked Villa.

"Same as ever, Unc. Just wait. And tomorrow we'll see if the forecast's right. If it is, I'll fly the time-keepers down to Adelaide and bring back their replacements."

He told Tonia his plans, too.

"You think it's wise to risk leaving the lake now, Donald?" she asked. "Just as soon as the plane takes off the wind's bound to drop. It's that sort of place."

"It's a risk we must take, sweetie. The time-keepers have all got jobs to get back to, and I can't keep them here forever without replacing them. There," he said, suddenly noticing the way she was looking. "You've been having too much of this damned place. Why don't you fly down with me for the ride? If the forecast's right and the wind has really set in for the next day or two, we'll spend the night in Adelaide, and bring the new time-keepers back the day after. A night in civilization will do us both good."

So the next morning when the camp awoke and the wind

showed no signs of abating, Campbell and Tonia and the time-keepers packed their bags and drove across to the blue and white plane on the edge of the dust-scoured runway. While the rest of the team was finishing breakfast, the Aero Commander climbed to six thousand feet and headed south for Adelaide.

Tonia was wrong about the wind. It showed no sign of dropping, not even to spite Campbell, and toward the end of the afternoon at Muloorina it gathered force and brought fresh rainclouds down from the north. Then while Tonia and Campbell slept in Adelaide, it rained, and early next morning when Villa and Norris drove out to inspect the track they found the whole southern end flooded, bringing the total length down to a mere ten and a half miles. Even this ten and a half miles was wet, the surface softened.

"My Lord, Ken," Villa said incredulously, as he squinted along the track. "The skipper's had it. We're back at the beginning again."

They drove back to the homestead and telephoned Campbell in Adelaide. It took some time for the call to get through and Campbell took the news philosophically, as he had learned to by now. It was Villa who seemed the more agitated of the two.

"It could take another month to dry out. Good Lord, yes. Another month. A month at least."

It was a bad line. The connection was not very clear and Villa was shouting for emphasis.

"If it does, it does, Unc," replied Campbell. "Take it easy. I'll fly back immediately. And what about the fresh time-keepers? No point in bringing them all the way to Muloorina now, I suppose? I'll send them back to Melbourne. See you soon."

Tonia was watching Campbell closely as he replaced the telephone. For several moments they looked at each other without speaking.

"Well?" she said finally.

"If Leo's right, it looks as if we've had it. I'd better go back to the lake, darling, but there's nothing for you up there now." He paused, looking at her anxious face. "If anything happens I'll telephone. You'll be better here for a few days with Florence."

It took longer for Campbell to get airborne from Adelaide than he expected, and longer still to make the flight back to Muloorina, so that it was nearly dark when he arrived and there was not time to visit the lake that day.

Not that there seemed any great need to do so. The facts were inescapable. Enough of his people had seen the effect of the rain to tell him what he needed to know. He held a small meeting straight away with Villa, Mustard, Norris, and the stewards, and all said the same thing. The three miles at the southern end of the track were completely unusable and what was left of the course would take at least a month to dry.

"Another postponement then, gentlemen?" Campbell said slowly.

No one answered.

"Well?" asked Campbell.

There was still a pause. Then Norris spoke. As usual he seemed reluctant to push himself forward and talked diffidently, looking down at the table in front of him.

"There's just a chance, Don, that the rain may have softened only the very surface of the track. The core of the salt underneath was pretty hard before the rain. When we have another look tomorrow we may find that it's stood up better than any of us think."

Campbell nodded. No one else spoke. What Norris had said seemed unlikely, but there was no harm in hoping.

"Very well then," said Campbell. "It looks as if everything depends on what we discover when we fly to the lake tomorrow morning."

But before then there was more he needed to know from Norris, and the next morning, immediately after breakfast, the two men strolled across from the homestead to Norris' trailer. It was a bright, windy day. Several of the white hens in the chicken run behind the homestead were in moult and they perched, melancholy, stranded creatures, sheltering their nakedness against the wind behind an old packing case for Stork margarine. Some of their feathers had stuck to the wire netting like tufts of very grimy cotton wool.

"Ken," said Campbell, "apart from this track, are you really satisfied with the car now?"

"As far as we've gone, perfectly. But there's still an awful lot we need to know. When you feel like giving me the rest of those test runs you promised me once, I'll have a clearer answer for you."

Campbell shook his head. "Sorry. No chance of that now, Ken. We're just going to wait here now for that one chance we need. I know we'll get it. And when it comes. *When* it comes, Ken. . . ." He stopped to emphasize what he was saying and the Price laundry flapped behind him in the breeze. "I'll take it and I'll gamble everything on it. It's the only way."

Norris nodded and the two of them walked on.

"One thing I must know," said Campbell. "If you were right last night and this ten and a half miles of track has not been damaged too badly, is it still going to be long enough for us to get the record?"

"I thought you'd be asking that sooner or later," Norris replied. "We'd better do some arithmetic and find out."

So the flight to the lake was delayed for half an hour while Norris and Campbell sat down at the small table in the trailer. Norris consulted notebooks, scribbled figures, and plotted several graphs. Campbell smoked his pipe, looked at the graphs, and asked a number of questions about the results. And when the sums were done Norris screwed them up into a ball, tossed them into the waste-paper basket beside the sink, and said, "Of course it's only possible *in theory*. Everything's going to depend on what we find out at the lake."

Campbell landed the plane near the stewards' tent at the northern end of the track. Villa and Norris were both with him, and when they took the Valiant and drove the length of the course, they found that the salt on the ten and a half miles seemed harder than anyone had dared hope. The southern end was still under water and a mile or so at the north was damp, but the center appeared to be nearly dry.

"Well, what d'you think, Unc?" asked Campbell, stamping on the salt with his heel. "Will it or won't it?"

"Hard to tell, Skipper. Ken could be right about that core of salt below the surface. It's dried far better than I ever thought it could. In a few days we might know the answer."

"A few days, eh?"

For a moment or two Campbell stood, hands in his pockets, staring silently along the track.

"Wind's nearly dropped, Don," said Norris. Campbell nodded.

"Unc," he said quietly. "How long before you can have the car running?"

"Ten minutes, Skipper. But why?"

209

"I want to know the answer about that track now, not in a few days' time, and there's only one sure way of finding out the truth. And would you ask George Hammond to set the turbine governors one hundred and ten percent power. Ken has a theory and we're going to try it out."

"So you tried the car with extra power, did you, Donald?" said Tonia when she met him at Adelaide airport. "You promised that you wouldn't drive Bluebird when I wasn't there."

Campbell was feeling pleased with himself; his one run had been more successful than he had dared hope. There was a chance again now, and he had flown straight to Adelaide from the lake to bring back Tonia and his fresh time-keepers.

"Sorry, darling, but it was one of those spur of the moment things that just had to be done. And it worked, sweetie. Worked like a charm. The acceleration was phenomenal."

He smiled at her, but she refused to smile back.

"That's not the point," she said sharply. "You know I don't interfere when you take these risks, but I must *know*, Donald. I must be there. That's always been our agreement and it's only fair." She saw then that he was still smiling. "What's so funny?" she said.

"It's just that this morning we found what could be the answer to all our troubles."

"How?" she said, relenting a little.

"I'll explain. You remember when we went for the record at the beginning of June and reached 389?"

She nodded.

"We were practically on maximum power and it was quite obvious that in the state the salt was in it just wasn't enough. Bluebird was having to plough its way through and it was like driving with the brake on. Now one of the reasons I

210

postponed the attempt for a month was in the hope we'd get a hard enough surface to avoid this. But just in case we didn't, I wanted another card up our sleeve. So when Ken was back in England I asked him to visit the research boys at Bristol Siddeley to see if we could increase the output of Bluebird's turbine beyond its hundred percent rating."

"What do you mean?" she said.

"Well, the output of a gas turbine is not limited in quite the same way as the output from a piston engine. You're really concerned with your safety margin. But for short periods, if you know what you're doing, it's perfectly possible to increase its power to more than a hundred percent."

"And what did these experts say to Ken?"

Campbell shrugged and stopped smiling. "They weren't terribly keen. But they finally agreed that if it ever became absolutely essential, we could increase Bluebird's power to a maximum of one hundred and ten percent. When the track was cut to eleven miles the other night I thought there would be nothing for it then but to wait on for another month or so until the rest of it dried again. But this morning Ken figured out that even with an eleven-mile track in the state ours is, it should still be possible to accelerate fast enough to pass through the measured mile at over 400."

Campbell was talking faster now. Tonia showed no sign of being reassured by what he was saying, but he did not seem to notice.

"There was only one condition," he said. "According to Ken's calculations, we needed a hundred and ten percent power on the turbine."

"And that's what you tested out without telling me this morning, was it?"

"Guilty, darling." He lit a cigarette and inhaled deeply. "But it was fantastic. She was up to 320 in little over a mile.

This is the answer we wanted all along. We're going to get it now, you know."

She realized then that he was in dead earnest. "I don't like the sound of it. You know the salt's not good, and the rain can't have helped matters, whatever you say. What's to stop you losing control as you did at Utah? You were accelerating hard then, don't forget."

"But I've learned a lot since then and I won't be breathing pure oxygen this time. Don't you realize it's either this or else hanging on here for another month or two, and then it'll probably rain again. It's a chance, darling. It's a chance and I've got to take it."

She knew then that she must not argue any more.

"When's it to be?" she asked.

"Soon as possible. I've rung Melbourne and the time-keepers are flying here this evening. We'll get back to the lake tomorrow morning."

He noticed then how pale she had gone and took her hand.

"Don't look so worried," he whispered. "In a day or two it'll all be over. D'you realize just what it will mean to us? Nothing else to worry about. We can both start living again then."

But the wind was still blowing when they got back to the lake, and although the whole Bluebird team was standing by for the rest of Thursday, the lull they needed never arrived. Evening came without the wind abating, but Campbell seemed quite unconcerned. Somehow he had convinced himself that his one chance was near and his confidence spread silently through the camp.

"Early start tomorrow, I'm afraid, Unc," he said, "but this will be the last of them. I'd like her rolling by 7:00."

"But what about the wind, Skipper?"

212

"The wind will be all right. The weather forecast says there'll be a period of calm and there's damn well going to be one. We've all put up with Lake Eyre long enough. Tomorrow's got to be the day."

"You know it's a Friday, don't you?"

"I don't care what day of the week tomorrow is, Unc, as long as it's the day we get the record. And Ken, one hundred and ten percent power."

Norris nodded and looked steadily at him. "One hundred and ten, Don."

"You realize it's going to be very close," said Norris. "The salt's far from ideal still, and once you're over 350 you're going to have your work cut out to stop those wheels spinning. So take her up to 350 at full throttle and then ease your foot back just a shade. You'll carry on accelerating, and that should take you through the mile at just over 400."

It was 7:10 on the morning of Friday, July 17th, and Campbell had just landed on the lake. For the first time since his return to Muloorina the wind had died away, and he was anxious to be off. The time-keepers had been in position for half an hour, the stewards were ready, the mechanics had completed their final check. It was cold and the salt underfoot felt like ice.

After his brief discussion with Norris, Campbell glanced toward the stewards' tent where the two red Dunlop flags hung motionless against the aluminum masts. Then without a word he took his helmet and his bear and his blue tennis shoes from Tonia and the start-up began.

"Unc," he said before the canopy closed. "I know it's Friday, but I'd just like you to make sure we don't start at 7:13. Seven-twenty's a good round number."

Norris and Villa took the gray Valiant and raced ahead of

213

Bluebird up the service road beside the track so that they were able to see the car streak past them like a blue rocket and hear the time-keeper's announcement over the car radio before they reached the end of the track.

"The speed through the measured mile was 403 miles an hour exactly."

"Nine miles an hour more than Cobb," said Norris.

"He's cutting it too close for my liking," said Villa and whistled through his teeth. "It's the return run that's the tricky one. He's got to accelerate now across the softest end of the track. I don't think he's going to do it, Ken."

When they reached Campbell he had opened the canopy already and taken off his helmet. He did not speak and his face was like a gray mask. The two and a half minutes it had taken him to get there had been enough to batter all the confidence and splendid impatience with which he had set out.

Swiftly, efficiently, the turn-around team began their work. Panels were removed, oil temperatures taken, and the yellow refueling truck backed noisily alongside.

"Well?" said Villa.

"It's no good, Leo. I nearly lost her. Just before the mile the wheels started spinning and I felt the tail begin to go. The wheels must have gone right through the surface. I never dreamed the track could be as bad as that."

"You think you chewed it up badly?"

"Must've done. We'll never be able to repair it."

"So what d'you want to do, Skipper?"

"I'll take her back on the other side of the blue line. It's our only chance. But I'm sorry, Leo. I think it's hopeless."

The car was swung around then. Campbell, grim-faced, silent, sat in the cockpit steering as the rest of the team pushed her backward and forward in a series of shallow arcs until Bluebird's nose was facing the way it had just come. Then the rams went down, the car raised herself up, and

214

the wheels were changed. Thirty-eight minutes after Bluebird had come to rest, she was ready to go again.

The atmosphere was tenser than it had ever been. There was nothing that anyone, not even Villa, could say now. However certain it might seem that Campbell was going to kill himself if he went on, no one could tell him to quit. Instinctively one tries to stop a man committing suicide, but now this was an instinct everyone had to fight down.

Campbell seemed to understand this himself, for we left him then and he waited in the cockpit, silent, completely alone, for the last few minutes to tick by.

Norris was one of the few people who saw what happened. He was standing by the cockpit, and noticed that Campbell was suddenly staring up at the perspex canopy in front of him. All the tension and strain seemed to have gone from his face. His eyes were open very wide. Then he suddenly took a deep breath, shut his eyes.

He stayed like this for a few seconds, his head on his chest. Then Leo Villa shouted from the booster truck, "We're okay, Skipper. Ready when you are," and Campbell opened his eyes and called back, "Fine, Leo," and the return run started.

For Campbell it must have been a terrifying journey. The track disintegrated at the third-mile mark, and he felt the wheels go through the surface of the salt. Any other time he would have taken his foot off the throttle, but now there was no going back and his foot stayed where it was on one hundred and ten percent power. The car began to vibrate as the razor-sharp salt started shredding rubber from the tires, and when he passed through the measured mile he had no idea whether he had made it or not.

He imagined not, for he was certain that the battering the car was getting from the salt must be slowing it down, and when the run was over and he lifted the canopy he sat there looking dejected.

It was one of Brebner's policemen who reached him first.

"Well done, Don, you've made it. Four hundred and three."

"Don't be stupid," said Campbell. "That was the first run. Find out what the real speed was. Not that it matters," he added.

Evan Green and Norris came up then.

"We missed it," said Campbell. "Our last chance on this track, and we missed it."

But then the policeman came back. He was shouting now and waving his arms excitedly.

"It is 403. I've checked with the time-keepers. Exactly 403 each way. It's the record, Don."

Campbell smiled, took off his helmet, and hoisted himself on the back of the cockpit. Somebody cheered, and the small crowd of people who had gathered around the car bore him away on their shoulders.

There was a barbecue that night by the army camp, and although Florence was still in Adelaide they brought her bottles of Great Western champagne out of the refrigerator and added a lot of others to them, and by 9:00 the geese and the pelicans and the rest of the birds along the creek were beginning to object to the noise.

It was a considerable party. Elliot Price was serving the drinks. The cameramen were feeling very pleased with themselves because they had finally finished their film. And happiest of all the party-goers were several carloads of people from Marree most of us had never seen before.

Soon people were dancing. More wood was thrown on the fire, immense shadows flickered, and the night air was sweet with the tang of wood smoke.

As a party the only strange thing about it was that it seemed to have so little to do with the people in whose

216

honor it was held. Villa and Norris were there, but they remained very much on the edge of things, and when Campbell finally arrived the party was already going with such a swing that no one seemed to notice him. He looked tired and lost and rather unhappy, and stood watching the party as if he could hardly understand what it was all about.

Elliot Price caught sight of him and came over to shake his hand.

"Well, Don, you've done it. I always knew you would. You've beaten Lake Eyre."

Campbell looked puzzled, then smiled tolerantly. "I suppose so, Elliot, though I can't quite believe it. Still feel a bit lost, to tell you the truth. But thanks for everything. You've been wonderful, Elliot. I'm very grateful." He shook hands again, and then walked over to Norris and Villa.

"Always the same, Skipper," said Villa. "The more of a struggle to win a bloody record, the more of a let-down when you've got it. I still can't believe in this one."

Campbell shook his head. "Nor can I, Unc. It's all over now. Let's forget it. I wanted to talk to you about the water record. The old boat's down in store in Adelaide. She's ten years old but I reckon she's still got a few extra miles an hour in her before we shove her in the museum. How's about getting on with it? No one's ever done the land and the water in one year."

For the next twenty minutes they talked, planning how they could win the water record—the choice of lakes, the transport problems, the supply of spares and food and fuel. Such talk seemed to bring the three men back to reality, and Campbell was about to leave the party when Norris asked him the question that had been puzzling him all day.

"Don," he said, "what happened this morning?"

"What d'you mean, Ken? When?"

"Between the two runs. When you were sitting there in the

cockpit waiting for the start, something happened to you, didn't it?"

There was a long pause. "Yes," said Campbell at last. "Something did happen. It was the most incredible thing I've ever experienced. You know what happened on that first run?"

Norris nodded.

"I nearly killed myself. I was so near going out of control that it wasn't even funny, and when I was sitting in the cockpit at the end of the run I really thought I had had it. For I knew the second run would be worse. I saw no hope at all.

"It was then that it was so extraordinary. You know how the canopy lifts up with the windscreen in front of the cockpit? Well, I suddenly looked up into it and there was my father reflected in the windscreen as clearly as you're sitting there now. I even recognized the white shirt and flannels he used to wear. For a few seconds he just looked at me, smiling. Then he said, 'Well boy. Now you know how *I* felt that time at Bonneville in 1935 when a front tire burst at 300. But don't worry. It'll be all right, boy.'

"Then he faded away."

Someone threw fresh branches on the fire, and as the smoke billowed up Campbell started coughing. It was probably the smoke that made his eyes water. He looked across at Villa, whose face had grown wise and golden and timeless in the firelight.

"There never was anyone like the old man, was there, Unc?" he said.

"No," replied Villa softly. "No one."